COUNTRY
WINES

To Make, Drink and Cook with

*There are two reasons for drinking; one is, when you are thirsty;
the other when you are not thirsty, to prevent it.*

THOMAS LOVE PEACOCK 1785–1866

COUNTRY WINES

To Make, Drink and Cook with

MOLLIE HARRIS
& HELEN PEACOCKE

ALAN SUTTON

First published in the United Kingdom in 1991
Alan Sutton Publishing Ltd · Phoenix Mill · Far Thrupp · Stroud
Gloucestershire

First published in the United States of America in 1991
Alan Sutton Publishing Inc · Wolfeboro Falls · NH 03896-0848

British Library Cataloguing in Publication Data

Harris, Mollie
Country wines to make, drink and cook with.
I. Title   II. Peacocke, Helen
641.872

ISBN 0-86299-992-8

Library of Congress Cataloging in Publication Data applied for

Jacket photographs: Front by Paul Felix; Back by Donald Coleman.

Colour sections photography: p. 1 Paul Felix; p. ii–xvi Helen Peacocke.

Line illustrations by Martin Latham.

Whilst every care has been taken to ensure that all measurements and details
given in the recipes are correct, the publishers cannot accept any responsibility
for inaccuracies or their consequences.

Typeset in 11/13 pt Bembo.
Typesetting and origination by
Alan Sutton Publishing Limited.
Colour separation by Yeo Graphics Reproductions Ltd.
Printed in Great Britain by
The Bath Press, Bath, Avon.

Contents

◇◇◇

CONTENTS

CONTENTS

CONTENTS

CONTENTS

CONTENTS

Introduction

Home-made wines have been made almost since time began. Man soon found out the value of using flowers, fruits, herbs and leaves to make them. In the first place – and for centuries – wines were just drunk for medicinal purposes.

Noah is believed to have been the first man to have planted a vineyard and to have concocted one of man's greatest blessings – the making of home-made wines. And in the book of Genesis it states that 'Noah drank the wine and was drunken'. But, most likely, he – like my grandparents and many old folk – just drank it for medicinal purposes. It probably tasted so good that he ended up having a 'skinful'.

Over the years, Roman emperors and Greek and Egyptian gods were all renowned wine drinkers. So it is not surprising that today more people than ever make wines from wild and garden flowers, fruit, herbs, leaves and vegetables – the list is endless. I reckon to make one, and sometimes two, sorts of wine every month, and this year concocted a new one, wallflowers and grapefruit. I had started to pull up the wallflowers to make way for the bedding plants, when I noticed that there were quite a few 'just out' flowers at the top of the plants. So I picked about a quart jug full, then sliced a couple of grapefruit up, poured boiling water over them and proceeded to make the wine in the usual way – and although I have not tried it yet, it looks lovely and is a pale pink colour.

And last year was a wonderful season for mulberries. A friend invited me to 'come and pick as many as you like'; she has a 300-year-old tree in her garden and it was loaded. If *you* ever get the chance to gather some sometimes, don't wear a white blouse or shirt! I was almost ashamed to walk down our village street after I had picked them – I looked as if I had just done a murder, and I got some very funny looks, I can tell you!

Making your own wine is so much cheaper than having to buy it; and then there is the satisfaction of having produced it yourself. You will find that your guests will really enjoy it when you offer them some with a meal or just as an apéritif, and of course you can use the wines in cooking.

This book is different: it is not just about how to make wines for drinking, it is also about how to *use them in cooking* – not only with the odd chicken, but with fish, meats, game and super puds.

Helen Peacocke, a young lady who lives in my village, has spent several years in Australia, but a few summers ago she came back to England – the whole country looked green and lush, the gardens and hedgerows filled with fruit and flowers – so different from the country she had just left. One of the first things she came across in one of the village shops was a book on home-made wines – one that I had just had published called *A Drop O'Wine* (now out of print). She bought it, read it, and was inspired. She thought – this is a bit of Old England, the simple way to make wine as our grandmothers and mothers made it, with straightforward recipes and ingredients that are easy to find.

She promptly set to and made all the wines in the book, which took her throughout the year. Now, Helen is a qualified cook, and for several years was a lecturer in a catering college in Australia. So she started experimenting using all sorts of her wines in a number of recipes, and has come up with a fascinating way to use many of them, thus producing simple, mouth-watering and unusual dishes.

Now Helen joins me in this book, which contains the best of those well-tried and loved home-made wines plus some exciting new concoctions, and Helen's tempting recipes. Of course, many of you will have made wines already, so you can start to cook with them straight away. But if you are a beginner, why not start now? First make your wines, and in a few months' time you will be able to drink them and, of course, cook with them. And then you can enjoy bountiful fruits, flowers and vegetables all the year round, many of which are there 'just for the picking'.

Mollie Harris

Starting Out

Wine-making can be inexpensive and *very* simple. If you need to go in for complicated and scientific processes, then this is no book for you. But I can assure you that it is possible for the beginner to produce good wines with the minimum of equipment and a little patience, and at half the cost of shop wines. It need not be time-consuming either – unless, of course, you want it to be. But the pleasure, pride and sense of achievement when you open that very first bottle is worth any effort involved. Then there are the friendships that wine-making can bring, competitions to enter, wine-tasting sessions in friends' homes, swapping hints and recipes and, above all, a wonderful feeling of satisfaction from the realization that you have produced a brain-tickling wine from something that you may well have thought to be a useless weed.

Keep your eyes open as you travel around, especially in the early spring, and note where the snowy white blackthorn blossom blooms – come late September or early October, there should be lots of lovely sharp blue-black sloe berries on the branches. Sloe wine is lovely, and sloe gin even better. Elderberries are easy to spot and very prolific, and grow almost everywhere in the autumn. And a sharp eye can notice where wild crab-apples hang like small lanterns on leafless trees in late autumn, and gorse a-blooming on common ground.

Throughout the year look out for stinging nettles, rose hips, the blossom and the leaves of the may bush. Even young oak and walnut leaves can be used for wine-making, while coltsfoot flowers make an excellent drink (for years in my extreme youth I was afraid to pick them – they were nicknamed 'pee the bed', and were supposed to make you do just that). Dandelions, of course, produce one of the nicest of wines, and my gramp swore by agrimony wine – agrimony is a tall yellow wild flower – for his rheumatics. Then there are all the garden fruit and vegetables, almost all of which can be used in wine-making.

Most of the things you need for wine-making you probably already have in your kitchen. For all *my* wine-making, I use an earthenware pan – it was my gran's, and very useful it is too – but a large white plastic bucket or a large bowl will do just as well.

Then you'll need a funnel, most probably of plastic. Never use anything tinny or iron-based, as an unpleasant flavour can be imparted into the wines; aluminium and glass are all right, however. And you will need a large jug, say a quart one, and muslin for straining the wine – I use a fine old nylon net-curtain which answers the purpose beautifully.

My only modern investment is a demijohn. For years and years I never bothered with one, but they are useful during fermentation, which is the next stage of wine-making. My daughter-in-law presented me with mine – she said that she was fed up with the sound of gunfire coming from my larder. You see, if you put wine straight into bottles the corks blow out, and she reckoned that to sit in our cottage was like being at the Battle of Waterloo. So she presented me with a demijohn and an airlock, and since then I have wondered how on earth I managed all those years without one. Now I own several.

You will also need a bung and an airlock which are fitted into the demijohn, a wooden spoon, a packet of paper filters, a small piece of plastic tubing to siphon the wine from the demijohn (not absolutely essential), a few campden tablets and, later on, some bottles complete with corks – and, *if* you can get hold of one, a good old-fashioned stone cask to store your wine in, before bottling it off.

Once you start making wine, think how often you will be able to enjoy the fruits of your labours – not only you, but your friends too. And there is a lot to be said for swapping tips and ideas over a glass of wine.

After you've made your first gallon of wine, don't just sit back waiting until it's fit to drink, but set about making different types, so that by the time the first lot is ready you will have a steady supply to follow.

TO MAKE THE WINE

To make all wine, the method is very much the same. Yeast and sugar are added to a mixture of juice and water: sometimes the water used is cold and poured over the main ingredients, sometimes boiling water is called for, and sometimes the ingredients are boiled. The enzyme in the yeast works the sugar and the yeast begins to breed, producing millions of little cells which live on the sugar, gradually turning your wine into alcohol and gas – the bubbles that are given off during the fermentation period.

Try to keep your working wine in a temperature of 65 °F – that's easy to do in the sumertime, but make sure that your winter wines don't get cold. Friends of mine keep theirs in the airing cupboard during the really cold weather.

The sweetness or dryness of wine depends on the amount of sugar you use in each batch: 2 lb 8 oz of sugar to each gallon of juice will produce a dry or medium-dry wine, while 3 lb 8 oz–4 lb will give you a lovely sweet wine. Always use granulated sugar unless otherwise stated. Should you get one that turns out too dry, or even one that turns out too sweet, not to worry – 'come drinking time', and you can always blend them with others to the dryness or sweetness that suits your palate.

For years I used solid baker's yeast which I bought from our local baker, an ounce at a time, when I needed it, and I still use it whenever I can. If the baker's is shut, then I use packets of bread yeast which serves the same purpose, although I know that not everyone agrees with this method. If you *must* buy special yeast, do so by all means, but I never do.

Soon after the yeast has been added, you will notice that an inch or two of froth will form on the top, which means that the wine is working well.

Always keep your wines covered with a thick cloth in the early stages) before they go into the demijohn); otherwise you might be plagued with wine flies, which seem to be able to detect home-made wine a mile off (although my brother, who once worked for a wine merchant, said that they had to watch out for them when they were bottling off some of their good wines). These flies are small and blackish-brown, and if they get into your wine they can quite easily turn a good wine sharp and sour, like vinegar – indeed some folks call them vinegar flies. You will also notice them flying around when you are decanting wine for drinking.

Once your wine is made, you should strain it and funnel it into your demijohn, which you should always fill (top it up with a little water if necessary). Fix in your bung and an airlock; the airlock should have a little water in it. Stand the demijohn on a tray and then place it in a fairly warm room – a kitchen is ideal.

After a while you will notice that the water in the airlock will, quite regularly emit a bubble, which means that your wine is working well. Leave it in the demijohn till this working has ceased – some wines take longer than others – and then bottle off, or put into a cask and leave to mature. Once you think that the wine is drinkable, the best thing to do is to decant it. Have some clean bottles ready, along with a funnel and some wine filter papers. Line the funnel with a filter paper and put it in the top of an empty bottle. Now pour or siphon the wine from the demijohn through the funnel and into the clean bottle; gradually it will drip through the filter, clearing it as it does so. Occasionally you will have to renew the filter paper when it becomes discoloured or the wine doesn't seem to be dripping through. This is a slow job and can be done in-between other jobs about the house. If, when you have decanted all the wine, it is not quite clear, leave it in the bottles for another few weeks, after which you may have to decant it again.

If you store your wine in casks rather than in bottles, you must be very careful when you come to decant it. There is bound to be some sediment at the bottom and you really don't want to keep this. If you just tip the cask up to get the wine out, the sediment will cloud all the wine. The best thing to do is to siphon off the wine from the sediment. For this you will need a piece of clean rubber or plastic tubing a quarter or half an inch in diameter. I simply suck mine up through the tube to get it started, but you can buy a special siphon tube or siphon pump, if you wish. Discard all sediment.

To make sure that your containers are clean and free from any bacteria, sterilize them, either with ordinary washing soda, using 4 oz to a gallon of boiling water, or crush 6 campden tablets in a pint of water (this mixture can be used again and again). You can also buy from most chemists small tubs of VWP Cleaner and Sterilizer, either in tablet or powder form, which is recommended for all home-brewing equipment.

Once a bottle of home-made wine has been opened it will keep indefinitely, unlike bought wines. And all wines improve with keeping. Always be sure that your wine is *cool*, but not *cold*, before adding the yeast.

Wine-making Problems and Cures

◇◇◇

It doesn't matter how good a wine-maker you are or how many years you have been at it, just occasionally one batch might not turn out as good as you expected it to. Provided you follow the instructions and recipes properly and your equipment has all been sterilized, all should be well. So what can go wrong?

LOSS OF COLOUR

Your beetroot, blackberry, sloe and elderberry wine should range in colour from red to burgundy. But if you leave it in a strong light for too long, the wine might lose some of the attractive colour. So keep fermenting wines away from direct strong sunlight, and if you must put them in a sunny window, then wrap several thicknesses of brown paper round the demijohns.

WINE TURNING INTO VINEGAR

This sometimes happens if you have not completely filled your jar (or whatever you keep your wine in after fermentation has stopped), or if the wine is kept in too damp and cold a place. A wise wine-maker should not run this risk. If the worst happens, try crushing a campden tablet and adding it to the jar, and leave it for a couple of days. If this doesn't do the trick, then it's probably too late to save the wine, but at least you will have a good supply of wine vinegar.

THINNESS

If your wine tastes thin and weak, then you haven't used enough fruit or vegetables – at least, not as much as the recipe states.

Sometimes when the recipe says, for example, 3 lb of plums, you may well weigh them stones and all – but after you have destoned them the end product will certainly be less than 3 lb. If you think your wine is thin, the best thing is to blend it with a thick one like, say, elderberry.

CLOUDINESS

Some wines in the early stage, and for no reason at all, can resemble pea soup, cloudy and awful to look at, and not all that nice to taste. The thing to do is bottle it off, store it away and forget about it for a year or longer. You will then find that most of the wrongs have been put right and you have bottles of clear, pleasant-tasting wine. Once I made some rose petal wine and it turned out so dry that no one wanted it. So I stored it away and forgot about it. Four years later I remembered it, fetched it out and by then somehow it had lost a deal of its dryness, and I was left with some *very* nice wine. But afterwards when I was telling the tale to a very experienced wine-maker, he said 'All you needed to do was to add half an ounce of glycerine to each pint of wine.'

Don't be put off with the things that *can* go wrong: follow the instructions properly and there is very little that time and common sense won't put right.

Handy Measurements

All wine-making recipes will make 1 gallon of wine; food recipes are for four people.

If the following are required for 1 Gallon	the working equivalent for 5 Litres will be
2 lb	1000 g or 1 kg
1 lb	500 g
8 oz	250 g
4 oz	125 g
2 oz	60 g
1 oz	30 g
$\frac{1}{2}$ oz	15 g
4 pints	2.5 litres
2 pints	1.25 litres
1 pint	600 ml
1 fluid oz	30 ml
$\frac{1}{2}$ fluid oz	15 ml

1 gallon equals 4.55 litres
2.2 lb equals 1 kg

GAS MARK	CELSIUS SCALE [°C]	FAHRENHEIT [°F]
$\frac{1}{4}$	110 °C	225 °F
$\frac{1}{2}$	130 °C	250 °F
1	140 °C	275 °F
2	150 °C	300 °F
3	170 °C	325 °F
4	180 °C	350 °F
5	190 °C	375 °F
6	200 °C	400 °F
7	220 °C	425 °F
8	230 °C	450 °F
9	240 °C	475 °F

Use granulated white sugar in these recipes unless demerara sugar is specified.

Country Wines to Make, Drink and Cook With

APPLE

Apple Wine

Apple wine can be made from late August until early October; and
for it you will need

> 8 lb windfall apples – cookers or eaters
> 1 gallon water
> 3 lb sugar
> $\frac{1}{2}$ oz yeast

Cut the apples up into small pieces; don't peel them, but cut out
any bad bits. Put them into your bucket or large bowl, pour the
water, cold, over them, sprinkle on the yeast. Cover with a cloth,
and leave for 4 days. Stir vigorously 2 or 3 times a day. After the
fourth day strain through your muslin or fine curtain, squeezing
well to get out all the juice. Tip the juice back into your bucket
and add the sugar. Cover well with a thick cloth, and leave in a
warmish place – the kitchen will do. Take a peep after a few hours
to see if it is working well. You can tell if it is, for it should have
an inch or two of froth on the top. This applies to *all* wines after
the yeast has been added. Leave in the bucket for about a week.
Strain again, tip it into your demijohn, and proceed as on page 4.

Watch this wine, as it is supposed to have aphrodisiac qualities.
A sweet delicate wine, it will be drinkable after 4 months.

Jellied Ham and Chicken with Apple Wine

1 bacon hock weighing at least 2 lb
1 small chicken, quartered but not boned
1 pint apple wine
Small bunch of mixed herbs to include cherville, tarragon,
  and parsley if possible
6 level teaspoons gelatine
Freshly ground black peppercorns and salt to season

Soak the ham overnight in cold water to reduce salt content and enhance flavour. Drain and wash the hock and place in a large saucepan along with the chicken. Add wine and enough water to cover the meat, but not more than 3 pints. Add herbs and bring to the boil, reducing the heat once boiling point has been reached. Simmer gently until the chicken has cooked and is falling off the bone.

At this stage remove the chicken and take the meat off the bone while the hock continues to simmer. Return the chicken bones to the pot and continue to cook until hock is also cooked – this will probably take another three quarters of an hour. When cooked, remove hock from pot and carefully strain the liquid into another saucepan. As you are looking for a very clear sauce, it may be best to strain through a muslin rag if you have one. At this stage you should have just 1½ pints of liquid in the new pot. Soak gelatine in a little water until it is soft and no granules remain. Add this to the stock and stir in well until it has completely dissolved and mixed in. Taste and adjust seasoning.

Chop meat into suitable chunks, or tear apart and leave in strips – either way is fine; it depends if you want a very neat finish or a rough country look. Pack the meat into a suitable container, adding if you wish a few freshly chopped herbs between the layers. These add a rather splendid colour-contrast to the finished dish. Pour stock onto the meat and cover, leaving to cool in the refrigerator until completely set. Do not attempt to cut this dish into portions until the gelatine mix has really set. Serve either as a first course or as the basis for a main meal.

Chicken Breasts Poached in Apple Wine and Cumin

¼ pint apple wine
4 chicken breasts, boned and skinned
2 firm cooking apples, peeled and sliced thin
*1 crisp red apple to use as garnish when the dish is
    completed*
1 level teaspoon cumin powder
Flour to dust chicken breasts before frying
*½ pint chicken stock, made the traditional way if possible
    (if you do have to cheat and use a stock cube, reduce the
    amount of seasoning you use or your guests will spend
    half the night asking for glasses of water)*
1 large onion, chopped very fine
2–3 tablespoons sunflower oil to fry chicken breasts
Freshly ground black peppercorns and salt to season

Flour chicken breasts, season well and fry gently in oil until they
are crisp and brown on both sides. Remove cooked chicken from
frying pan and place in a large casserole. Lower the heat of the oil
and add the cooking apples and onions to the frying pan and cook
gently until soft but not brown. Raise the heat slightly and add
cumin powder and allow its flavours to explode. Then, without
wasting a moment, slurp in a generous amount of wine and allow
the mix to simmer gently for a moment.

Add rest of the wine and chicken stock, simmer again, taste,
adjust seasoning and pour the sauce complete with apples and
onions on to the chicken breasts. Cook in a moderate oven for
about 40 minutes – longer at a slower heat is even better if you can
spare the time, for like most dishes which contain spice – the
longer and the slower that they are allowed to cook, the fuller the
flavour. When cooked, garnish the finished dish with slices of red
apple. Do not overdo the garnish, you are aiming to enhance the
general appearance not cover the complete dish.

APRICOT

Apricot Wine from Fresh Fruit

◇◇◇

Here is a wine for fresh apricots – if you ever have enough to spare to make into a wine, it is absolutely delicious. But I only use the small ones for it.

> 6 lb fresh apricots
> 1 gallon boiling water
> 3 lb sugar
> ½ oz yeast

Place the apricots in your bucket and with both hands squeeze the fruit until it is quite pulpy, removing the stones at the same time. Pour over the boiling water. Cover and leave in a warm place for a couple of days. Strain, and tip back into your bucket. Add the sugar, stir well, then add the yeast. Cover and leave for a further 4 days. Strain again, tip it all into your demijohn, and proceed as on page 4.

This is a beautiful, golden-coloured wine with a delicate bouquet, and will be drinkable after 6 months.

Filo Pastry Dainties with Apricot Wine Filling

1 packet filo pastry
1 packet dried apricots (select the type that require overnight soaking)
2 oz sliced almonds
4 oz unsalted butter
Generous amount of apricot wine
1 teaspoon arrowroot to thicken sauce
Double cream to accompany dish

Soak the dried apricots in apricot wine overnight. Next day prepare flat baking tins for pastries by buttering carefully and then dusting with flour – this will stop the pastries sticking to the tray. Drain apricots very well, reserving the wine for the sauce, then melt the butter very gently so that it becomes a liquid but does not brown. Unpack filo pastry, taking great care to keep unused sheets covered to avoid them drying out. Lay out the first sheet of filo pastry and using a pastry brush carefully cover with butter. Place second sheet of filo on top of first buttered sheet and repeat process again. You are aiming for a total of 3 sheets, one on top of the other, all buttered.

Cut pastry into 2-inch squares. You can usually get 8 squares from each batch of sheets, so cut in half, and then each half in half again, then make a vertical stroke dividing the filo into eight equal squares. Place a teaspoon of sliced almonds in centre of each square and a well-drained apricot onto each pile of almonds.

Carefully bring opposite corners of each square together and allow them to bunch up at the top before bringing second corners together to form a shape that resembles an old-fashioned lavender bag that has been frilled at the top. The moist butter keeps them together. Place each pastry on buttered tray. Check that the outer edges are buttered to avoid the pastry burning and cook very, very gently until they turn a soft golden brown. Dust with icing sugar and eat hot with apricot sauce.

APRICOT SAUCE

Bring remaining wine to the boil and thicken with arrowroot, which has been thinned down with a little wine and gently stirred into the bubbling liquid until a reasonably thick sauce develops. The sauce can either be placed alongside the pastries on individual plates with the cream, or offered in a separate dish. Either way, these pastries are delicious and can be enjoyed hot or cold.

I love the taste of fresh apricots so much that somehow I never have enough fresh apricots to make into wine, so I have to rely on Mollie's wine store when I need a drop or two for my filo pastries.

APRICOT AND RAISIN

Apricot and Raisin Wine

This is a nice wine to make for those who cannot get into the country, and it can be made at any time throughout the year.

> *2 lb dried apricots*
> *1 lb raisins (chopped)*
> *1 gallon water*
> *2 lb 8 oz–3 lb sugar (depending on how sweet you want it)*
> *½ oz yeast*

Chop up the apricots quite small and soak overnight in cold water, just enough to cover the fruit. Next day tip this into your bucket or bowl and pour over it a gallon of boiling water. Cover with a thick cloth and leave for 3 days. Add the sugar and chopped raisins, stirring with a wooden spoon till all has dissolved. Sprinkle the yeast on top, cover and leave for a week. Strain into the demijohn, and proceed as on page 4. This makes a delightful, sweet wine, drinkable within 5 months.

Babas Soaked in Apricot and Raisin Wine

1 oz fresh yeast or a level tablespoon dried yeast
6 tablespoons warm milk (not boiled)
8 oz plain flour
4 large eggs, beaten well
2 oz caster sugar
4 oz soft butter
Generous quantity fresh cream whipped thick to fill cooked babas
Generous amount apricot and raisin wine to soak babas and add final flavour
A little oil and flour to prepare baba tins and prevent sticking

Prepare baba tins by rubbing with oil and dusting with flour. Mix yeast with warm milk, 2 tablespoons of flour and a teaspoon of the sugar and stir together well. Leave this mix to ferment in a warm place for at least 20 minutes. Place all other ingredients into a large mixing bowl and mix well together. Add fermented liquid and stir in well – beat for a few moments. Half fill each baba tin with this mix and place them in a warm area of the kitchen and leave them covered with a clean cloth until the mixture has started to work and they are at least two-thirds full.

Place in a reasonably hot oven – 400 °F for 15 minutes or until they are firm to the touch, yet soft and spongy inside. Place the babas onto a cooling rack which has been positioned over a container that will catch the drips as you pour wine over the cooked babas. (This way you waste nothing.) For this particular dish you are aiming for a moist spongy baba which is almost wet to the touch. (If you do not wish to add this much wine to a cake which is being served in the middle of the afternoon, you can thin down the wine with a little sugar syrup and pour that mix over instead.) When the babas have cooled completely, cut an insert in the top and fill with whipped cream and serve with a nice cup of tea.

Babas can actually be soaked in any rich wine; I have chosen apricot for this recipe because I like the taste, but I could have equally well used a wheat and raisin, or Mollie's special elderberry with raisins.

I often garnish the babas with slices of fresh fruit, or raspberries for extra taste and to balance the sweetness, but this depends on whom I have invited to tea.

BARLEY

Barley Wine

This is best made in February or March, and at that time of the year some of us have got a lot of little 'taters' left. Here is a good way of using them up.

> 1 lb old potatoes
> 1 lb washed raisins
> 3 lb demerara sugar
> 1 lb barley (begged from a farmer)
> $\frac{1}{2}$ oz yeast
> 1 gallon water

Scrub the potatoes, cut them up quite small, and put them into your wine-making container. Add the sugar. Then add barley and raisins, which I put through a very coarse mincer. (An old recipe I used once said to crush your barley: I did so, and it shot all over the kitchen, so I find that mincing the barley and raisins together is the best plan.) Add the gallon of boiling water and stir until you feel all the sugar has dissolved. When the wine is cool, add the yeast. Cover very closely for 3 or 4 days. Then strain, put into your demijohn and fix the airlock. Proceed as on page 4. Usually quite a lot of deposit forms in your jar after a few days, in which case siphon the wine off into another demijohn, fix the airlock and leave it to get on with the fermenting, which will take 4 or 5 weeks. Bottle off when all movement has stopped.

If left to mature for a couple of years, this wine tastes almost like whisky – but it can be drunk within 6 months. Good for sufferers from bronchitis and asthma.

Fillet Steak Finished in a Rich Barley Wine Sauce

4 fillet steaks, trimmed and flattened just a little
4 oz musrooms, sliced really thin
4 shallots or 1 large onion, sliced as thin as the mushrooms
2 cloves garlic, chopped so fine they almost become a paste
¼ pint rich barley wine
2 tablespoons sunflower oil to fry steaks
4 sprigs parsley or watercress to garnish finished dish
Freshly ground black peppercorns and salt to season

Rub garlic well into both sides of the steaks and season them well. Heat the oil in a frying pan until it almost bursts into flames – you are aiming to cook the outside of the steaks sufficiently while leaving a pink flesh inside and only quick cooking will really achieve this. Add steaks to the hot fat and cook quickly so that each side becomes crispy brown yet they remain spongy to the touch. Remove and keep warm while you prepare the sauce.

To the remaining fat in the frying pan add mushrooms and shallots and fry gently at a moderate heat until they are soft but not brown. Increase heat a little and add the wine and allow to bubble furiously. You are aiming to reduce the volume of the liquid by at least a third, and this is done by aggressive bubbling for a few moments without a lid on the pan. Lower the heat, taste and adjust seasoning. Return the steaks to the pan for just long enough to bring back to full heat and serve immediately with green garnish.

As the sauce in this dish is rich, I usually serve a very simple salad and crusty bread as the main accompaniment – the bread soaks up the sauce perfectly.

Christmas Mincemeat with Rich Barley Wine

1 lb currants
1 lb sultanas
1 lb raisins
3 crisp cooking apples, grated fine
Rind of 2 lemons and 2 oranges
4 teaspoons ground allspice
4 oz of suet (optional – I do not use it as I am then free to
  offer my mince pies to the many vegetarians who visit me
  during the Christmas season. The mix is so lush and
  juicy that suet is really an extra that can be ignored.)
2–3 cups rich barley wine

Simply tip all the ingredients except the wine into a large mixing bowl and stir well. Gradually add the wine. You are aiming for a reasonably slushy mix, as the fruit will gradually absorb the wine during the next few days. Stir well again – get the family to join in and make a wish if you want to be really traditional. Cover the bowl and leave for a day before stirring again.

Continue to stir mix once a day for at least a week or until the apples begin to break down and the flavours begin to blend together. Check that the mixture is settling down and has enough moisture, and add more wine if needed until the fruits are plump and juicy. Then bottle and store in a cool place until needed.

This mixture makes a very good mixer when you are cooking apple pies and want to pep them up a little.

24

BEETROOT

Beetroot Wine

This is best made in December or January.

> 4 lb beetroot or 2 lb beetroot and 2 lb parsnips
> 1 gallon water
> 3 lb demerara sugar
> 2 lemons
> $\frac{1}{2}$ oz root ginger
> 4 cloves
> $\frac{1}{2}$ oz yeast
> 1 wineglass brandy (optional)

Scrub the beetroot clean and cut up into small pieces. Place in a saucepan with the ginger and cloves, and cover with the water. Cook until tender but not mushy. Strain off the liquid into a large bowl or bucket. Add the sugar and the lemon juice and stir until all the sugar has dissolved. Add the yeast when the liquid is cool. Cover with a cloth and leave for 4 days. Strain through muslin, pour into a demijohn, and then proceed as on page 4. Keep the wine out of strong sunlight, as that will take the colour out of it – it's a good idea to wrap your demijohn round with brown paper. After it has stopped working, strain off your wine into jars, bottles or a cask.

Beetroot wine is especially good for anaemia.

This wine is much better if kept a year or more – it improves a great deal with age – and is even better if a wineglass of brandy is added just before bottling it off (this will produce a full-bodied wine).

A different tasting wine, drier and more potent, can be made by using 2 lb of beetroot and 2 lb of parsnips in place of the 4 lb of beetroot. Prepare the parsnips in the same way as the beetroot.

Do be sure to wash the beetroot *very* well before making your wine. One woman complained that hers tasted earthy – probably because she had not washed the beetroot well.

Bortsch Finished with Beetroot Wine

1 large onion, chopped fine
2 large uncooked beetroot, sliced just a little larger than
    matchsticks
2 large carrots, sliced the same way as the beetroot
4 stalks celery, sliced as matchsticks
1 green pepper, sliced thin
8 oz tomatoes, skinned and chopped fine
1 clove garlic, crushed or chopped very fine
3 pints meaty stock, preferably home-made (if you do use a
    stock cube, adjust seasoning)
$\frac{1}{2}$ pint beetroot wine
1 bay leaf
6 sprigs parsley and a little fresh thyme, chopped fine
3 cloves
Juice of 1 lemon
$\frac{1}{4}$ pint sour cream
2 tablespoons sunflower oil to fry vegetables
Freshly ground black peppercorns and salt to season

Heat the oil in a large pan and gently fry the vegetables, herbs and garlic until soft but not brown. Add wine and allow to bubble for a few moments. Add stock, bring to the boil again and adjust seasoning. Cloves can be added at this stage in a muslin bag so that they can be retrieved later without trouble.

Allow this soup to simmer for as long as possible – you will know by its taste when it is ready to eat. The flavour will actually improve if you have time to allow it to stand overnight, but be sure to keep it refrigerated if you intend to leave it longer than a few hours. Check seasoning again towards the end of its cooking period and add the lemon juice before serving with whipped sour cream. (This can be placed either in a side dish so that guests can help themselves or served up by spooning a little onto each dish of soup at the end.) Hot crusty garlic bread goes very well with this soup.

Bortsch is a thick soup which originated in Russia, but has now become as firmly established on the British menu as minestrone or French onion. Like so many classic recipes, there are several ways of cooking this dish and each one is as interesting as the next.

It became a firm favourite of mine when I realized that the Russians often added wine to their Bortsch – and what could be more natural than to add a splash or two of beetroot wine to a thick soup with a beetroot base? I experimented once or twice and came up with the recipe above, though I do sometimes add chunks of meat to this dish during the winter so that it becomes a real meal in itself.

Mullet Broth with Beetroot Wine

4 mullet weighing approximately 6 oz each
½ pint beetroot wine
2 pints fish stock, made from bones and skin of fish
1 bunch parsley, choppped fine
2 sprigs thyme, chopped fine
2 sprigs marjoram, chopped fine
Small bunch cherville, chopped fine
*4 anchovies, chopped roughly (remember to reduce the
    amount of salt in this dish as the anchovies will contribute
    a great deal of salt)*
2 medium onions, chopped fine
Juice of half a lemon
1 oz butter
Nutmeg to grate over finished dish
Freshly ground black peppercorns and salt to season

Wash and prepare the fish, and simmer for at least 15 minutes in
the fish stock. Remove the fish from liquid and bring it to the boil.
Allow stock to continue boiling until it has reduced by at least
half. Adjust seasoning. Using a large pan, cook the onions gently
in the melted butter, avoiding a high heat or any browning of the
butter or onions. Squeeze the lemon juice into onions, and then
add both the wine, fish stock and anchovies.

Bring the whole lot to the boil before adding the herbs and flesh
from the cooked mullet. Allow the lot to cook for a further
20 minutes over a gentle heat. Grate a little nutmeg on top of
finished dish. Serve as a thick soup in deep dishes and provide lots
of fresh crusty bread to mop up the juice.

This ancient dish has changed very little over the centuries. It
was particularly popular in the seventeenth century, though the
wine used then would have been referred to as sack or Canary and
would certainly not have been made from vegetables.

BLACKBERRY

Blackberry Wine

One of my favourite wines is blackberry, and my idea of spending a really lovely time is to go off on a balmy early autumn day to gather them. For the trip you need to be wearing sensible shoes and slacks, and go armed with a nice wicker basket and a walking stick to drag down the berries that seem almost out of reach. Pick the best of the fruit – you really don't want over-ripe ones. If you gather yours from the roadside, a quick wipe in a clean tea-towel should remove the dust and dirt: but try *not* to gather fruit or flowers from a busy roadside.

You can make this wine from mid-August until mid-October. It is so simple to make, and you will need

> *4 lb ripe blackberries*
> *1 gallon water*
> *3 lb sugar (or 2 lb 8 oz for a drier wine)*
> *1 oz yeast*
> *6 oz raisins (for a sweeter wine)*

Roll the berries very gently in a tea-towel to remove the dust, but don't wash them on any account. Place them in a large bowl or bucket and pour over them a gallon of boiling water. Cover with a cloth and leave for 3 days, stirring a couple of times each day.

Strain the liquid on to the sugar and stir well until you feel it has all dissolved. Leave for half an hour, and then add the yeast and cover closely. Leave in the container for a further 6 days. Then strain, put into the demijohn, and proceed as on page 4.

The wine should be ready to drink when 6 months old. Should you need a really sweet wine to serve with your sweet, add 6 oz of raisins when you add the boiling water. For a specially dry wine, use only 2 lb 4 oz of sugar and *no* raisins.

Only pick blackberries from brambles that are too high for a dog to cock his leg on. And never pick them after 12 October, for after that date *the devil piddles on them*.

Wood Pigeon Braised with Blackberry Wine and Blackberries

2 wood pigeons
½ pint blackberry wine
8 oz fresh blackberries
8 oz mushrooms, chopped fine; a few whole for garnish
1 clove garlic, chopped very fine
2 medium onions, chopped fine
2 tablespoons sunflower oil to fry wood pigeons
Flour to dust birds before frying
Freshly ground black peppercorns and salt to season

Wash pigeons well and cut in half, removing as many bones as possible, then dry on kitchen paper and dust with small quantity of seasoned flour. Fry pigeons in large shallow pan, turning and watching carefully until they are a deep golden brown, but not cooked through. Place half the blackberries at the bottom of a casserole dish, lay pigeon portions on top.

In the oil and juices that remain in the pan gently fry off the onions, mushrooms, garlic and parsley until soft but not brown. Add a small quantity of flour to this mix and stir in well before adding the wine gradually, stirring all the time. Once you have achieved a reasonably thin sauce, adjust seasoning and allow to bubble for a moment before pouring the mixture onto the ingredients in the casserole dish. Place the remaining blackberries on top (reserving just a few for garnish).

Cook in medium oven for at least 1½ hours to allow the meat to cook and the flavours to fuse together. Adjust seasoning. Fry off the remaining mushrooms and keep warm. Garnish the finished dish with uncooked blackberries and the mushrooms. An extra garnish of fried-bread triangles can be added if you wish.

As wood pigeons are considered to be at their best between the months of May and October, this is an ideal autumn dish to prepare with the first wild blackberries.

The Devil's Story

The story goes that, on 12 October many years ago, the Devil was trying to get into heaven and St Peter, who was guarding the pearly gates wouldn't let him in. The Devil then started to shout and demand entry. St Peter, fed up with this unwelcome visitor, gave the Devil a good shove and he went plummeting down to earth and landed in a great big blackberry bush. Badly prickled, the Devil cursed and swore and proceeded to piddle all over the blackberries – which sent them mouldy. And thereafter, all blackberries began to go mouldy around 12 October and so they shouldn't be eaten for fear of upsetting the stomach.

BLACKCURRANT

Blackcurrant Wine

The next two wines are lovely ones. I am fortunate to have both sorts of fruit in my garden, but you can easily go to a 'Pick Your Own' for them. The time to make blackcurrant wine is with the fresh fruit in July and August. However, blackcurrants can be frozen successfully, in which case you can make it at your leisure.

This wine is made a little differently from most, and for it you need

> *3 lb blackcurrants*
> *3 lb 8 oz sugar*
> *1 gallon water*
> *½ oz yeast*

Remove the stalks from the blackcurrants and roll the fruit in a clean tea-towel. Place the blackcurrants in a large bowl or bucket. Boil the sugar and water up together and pour at once over the fruit. Leave until cool, but not cold, before sprinkling on the yeast. Cover closely and keep in a fairly warm place for 5 or 6 days. Strain, put into a demijohn, and continue as on page 4.

Blackcurrant wine is especially good for colds and coughs. Warm gently, almost to boiling point, and drink it hot – preferably in bed. It tastes deliciously of blackcurrants, is lovely served with your sweet, and is drinkable after 6 months.

Blackcurrant Jelly Dessert with Blackcurrant Wine

◇◇◇

1 lb ripe blackcurrants
1 pint water
4 oz caster sugar (only use more if the dish is not sweet
  enough on tasting)
4 oz powdered gelatine
4 tablespoons blackcurrant wine
Fruit to decorate

Place the fruit into a saucepan along with the water and gently bring to the boil. Reduce to simmer and allow the fruit to cook until very soft. Remove from heat and when cool enough to handle pour through a jelly cloth which has been secured on a chair leg or some item of furniture which will permit you to place a large bowl underneath to catch the liquid. When all the liquid has been strained into a container, pour it into another saucepan with sugar and wine and heat through so that the sugar melts. Taste; only add more sugar if really needed.

Remove from heat and allow to stand while you mix the gelatine in a small amount of wine to soften. When gelatine has completely softened and all powder has been mixed into the liquid add to the main mix and stir well. Pour into a jelly mould and leave in a cool place to set.

Warming the mould slightly by gently immersing it into a bowl of warm water will help ease the finished jelly out so that it does not stick, but don't overdo the heat of the water or the length of time it is immersed – a moment is usually enough.

Decorate with fresh fruits. Frosted blackcurrants dipped first in egg white and then caster sugar always looks effective.

Blackcurrant Upside-down Pudding

◇◇◇

1 lb blackcurrants
½ pint blackcurrant wine
6 oz self-raising flour
4 oz margarine
4 oz caster sugar for pudding mix
2 oz granulated sugar to sweeten fruit
2 eggs – beaten well
1 tablespoon arrowroot

Place blackcurrant wine and blackcurrants into large saucepan and gently simmer until they are cooked. Add as much sugar as is needed to acquire a rich flavour – the actual amount will depend upon how much sun the blackcurrants were exposed to while ripening. Remove blackcurrants from heat, strain, retaining the liquid and leaving the fruit to cool. Place cool blackcurrants at the bottom of a seven-inch cake tin and proceed to make sponge.

Sponge is made by creaming together the margarine and sugar until light and fluffy. Add in beaten eggs and cream again. Fold in the flour gradually, adding a little milk if the mix is not thin enough. Spoon the sponge mix on top of the blackcurrants and cook at 350 °F for about 20 minutes or until the sponge springs back when touched in the middle. (Do not open the oven door for at least 10 minutes or the mix may flop through lack of heat.)

With the remaining juices make sauce by bringing juice to the boil and adding diluted arrowroot mixed with wine. Turn the cooked pudding upside down so that the blackcurrants are on the top. Pour the sauce onto the cake so that it soaks in and runs all down the sides in a succulent manner. Serve with whipped cream or yoghurt.

BRAMBLE TIP

Bramble Tip Wine

Look out for the new leaf growth on the blackberry brambles in April and May, for this wine is best made in the spring when the young bramble shoots are tender. Pinch them off the top of the stalks with your finger and thumb – there shouldn't be too many thorns early in the year.

> *4 lb bramble or blackberry shoots*
> *1 lb raisins*
> *1 gallon water*
> *1 lemon*
> *2 lb 8 oz sugar*
> *$\frac{1}{2}$ oz yeast*

Chop up the tips and then boil them up in the gallon of water for about half an hour. Strain off into a large bowl or bucket. Add the chopped raisins, sugar, and grated lemon rind and juice. Stir, then leave to get cool before adding the yeast. Cover closely and leave for at least 5 days before straining into the demijohn; then proceed as on page 4.

This will make a medium-dry wine, drinkable within 6 months.

Bramble Tip Wine Syllabub

1 pint rich Jersey cream
Approximately half a cup of bramble tip wine (quantity of
wine in this dish varies according to the thickness of the
cream used)
2 really fresh lemons with good clear skins
Caster sugar to taste (amount will vary according to
strength of the other ingredients)
Grated chocolate to garnish (optional)
Sweet biscuits to serve with finished syllabub

Whip the cream until it is almost as thick as it will go, then grate the skin of 1 lemon into this mix. Squeeze in juice of the lemon and stir well. Add 2 dessertspoons caster sugar and stir well. Drip wine into cream mix, beating all the time.

At this stage, stop and taste. You are trying to achieve a perfect balance of flavour and texture. This is done by instinctively adding just enough wine, sugar, and lemon rind and juice for the mixture to hold without becoming liquid. It should provide through the ingredients a perfect harmony of tastes.

If you do accidentally add too much wine, don't worry. Just pop out and get a little more cream, whip that up and add the liquid mix you have just made to the cream very gradually. (Yes, this is trial and error and no written recipe can really help you during the final stages – in the end this one is really up to you.)

This dish (or something very similar) was a firm favourite with seventeenth-century cooks who made it with cider and warm milk straight from the cow. Today, to add a touch of twentieth-century magic, I usually garnish with grated chocolate and serve chilled in a frosted glass with a sweetened biscuit.

BROAD BEAN

Broad Bean Wine

At some time or other most gardeners end up with a quantity of broad beans – probably in excess of those needed for seed – but I don't like eating them when they are what our gramp called 'pitch-eyed', otherwise old and hard. But a delightful dry wine can be made from them, and what you will need is

> *4 lb old broad beans (after they have been shelled)*
> *4 oz sultanas*
> *1 lemon*
> *1 gallon water*
> *3 lb sugar*
> *½ oz yeast*

Shell the beans and simmer them in the water for about an hour. Strain the liquor off into a large bowl or bucket and add the chopped sultanas, lemon juice and sugar. Stir well until the sugar has dissolved. Add the yeast when the wine is cool but not cold. Cover with a thick cloth and leave for 6 days. Strain into your demijohn, fix the airlock, then proceed as on page 4.

This makes a nice amber-coloured dry wine; it can be drunk when 6 months old but is best left for a year.

Broad Beans in Broad Bean Wine Sauce

3 lb unshelled broad beans or 1 lb shelled
4 rashers streaky bacon without rind – roughly chopped
1 small onion, finely chopped
1 bunch parsley, finely chopped
4 tablespoons broad bean wine
½ pint milk
3 tablespoons flour
2 oz butter
Freshly ground black peppercorns and salt to season

In a saucepan of salted water boil the broad beans until cooked – this will not take very long if they are picked straight from the garden and are tender.

While they are cooking prepare the sauce. Melt the butter in a saucepan and gently fry the bacon pieces. Before it cooks too much and turns brown, add the flour and stir well. To this paste gradually add the milk a little at a time, stirring throughout until you have achieved a good sauce. Pour in the wine and stir. Add the chopped parsley and adjust seasoning.

When the beans are cooked, add them to the sauce and serve with a main dish which allows the beans to be the dominant flavour of the meal.

CARROT

Carrot Wine Made with Young Carrots

This wine hasn't got the maturity of wine made with old carrots, but it is quite nice.

> *4 lb carrots*
> *4 lb sugar*
> *1 gallon water*
> *Juice and rind of 2 lemons and 2 oranges*
> *1 oz yeast*

Scrub the carrots, after cutting off the green tops and tails. Slice them and place in a large saucepan along with the water, and boil until tender. Strain the liquid onto the sugar and add the juice and rinds of the lemons and oranges. When cold add the yeast. Cover with a thick cloth and leave for about a week. Then strain off and pour the liquid into your demijohn. Fix the airlock and proceed as on page 4. Leave at least a year before drinking.

Carrot Wine

Now use old carrots for this wine. A good time to make it is February or March when they are really mature.

4 lb carrots (without the green tops)
4 lb demerara sugar
1 gallon water
Juice of 2 grapefruit and 2 oranges
1 oz root ginger
1 oz yeast

Scrub the carrots but don't peel them. Slice them quite thinly and put them into a large saucepan. Add the water and crushed ginger and boil until the carrots are *quite* tender. Strain the liquid onto the sugar and stir well, then leave to cool. Add the fruit juices and yeast. Cover with a cloth and leave for a week. Then strain off into your demijohn, fix the airlock and proceed as on page 4.

Carrot wine is reputed to be very good for gout sufferers, but also makes an excellent wine to serve with your main meal. It is best left for 10 months before drinking.

Chicken with Peach and Carrot Wine Sauce

4 chicken breasts
1 bunch spring onions, chopped fine
1 small can of peaches
6 large carrots, chopped fine
6 sprigs parsley, chopped fine
1 oz fresh ginger, chopped fine
½ pint carrot wine
1 bunch watercress, to garnish finished dish
2 dessertspoons sunflower oil
Flour to dust chicken portions
Freshly ground black peppercorns and salt to season

Dust chicken portions with seasoned flour. Heat oil in large frying pan and fry chicken breasts until golden brown and cooked right through. Remove chicken from pan and keep warm while you make the sauce. Strain the liquid from the peaches and set four peach portions aside for final garnish.

In the juices that remain in the frying pan, fry off the carrots, chopped ginger, spring onions and parsley until carrots are soft. This can be achieved easily by placing a lid on the pan after you have exposed the mix to the first flush of heat. Place the remaining peach portions in blender and pulp, add the cooked mix of vegetables and herbs and blend again until you have a soft sauce. Return the mix to the pan and reheat.

Add the wine and stir well – this should thin down the mix to a fine sauce which will pour easily. Slice chicken breasts so that they fan out attractively. Pour a good quantity of sauce onto each plate and place chicken breast on top, then garnish with watercress and a whole peach portion.

This is a very sweet dish, but goes well with freshly minted new potatoes and a crisp summer salad.

CHERRY

Cherry Wine

Made with cherries when at their best, this will produce a lovely rich fruity wine.

> 1 quart black cherries
> 4 lb sugar
> 3 quarts cold water
> 1 quart pale ale
> Sprinkling of yeast

Measure the cherries in a jug, prick each one with a needle. Tip all the ingredients into your bowl or bucket, stir well and cover with a thick cloth. Stand in a warm room for about 2 weeks, then strain the wine into your demijohn, fix the airlock and continue as on page 4.

Cherry wine improves with keeping, so try not to use for a year. Don't throw away the strained cherries as they make quite a nice pie filling.

Cherry Tartlets with Cherry Wine

1 lb ripe succulent cherries, stoned
¼ pint cherry wine
1 teaspoon arrowroot or cornflour
6 oz wholemeal flour
4 oz unsalted butter
2 oz flaked almonds
Raspberry, cherry or strawberry jam
2 oz flaked almonds

Prepare traditional shortcrust pastry by mixing together flour and butter which, when rubbed together, resembles breadcrumbs. Add sufficient water to the mix to form a firm paste, then roll out pastry and cut into rounds that will fit your favourite tartlet tins.

Bake the tartlets in a moderate oven without a filling, having marked each one with a fork on the bottom to prevent the dough from rising during the cooking. It is worth checking the tartlet cases half way through and if necessary pressing the pastry down in the middle if it is beginning to rise up a little. (Do this job quickly before the oven or the pastry loses its heat.)

Place a spoonful of jam at the bottom of each cooked tartlet and then fill the case with as many cherries as will fit comfortably. Place the wine in a small saucepan and bring to the boil, adding arrowroot or cornflour that has been diluted with a little wine to thicken the sauce. Stir continually while you add this to the wine. When a good clear sauce has been achieved carefully spoon a little of the wine sauce onto each tartlet, covering the cherries completely if possible. Garnish with flaked almonds.

Cherry Cream with Cherry Wine

1 pint thick Jersey cream (this dish really does need a good
*   quality cream to bring out its true flavour)*
1 lb ripe red cherries picked while the sun is still on them
*   and they are bursting with juice*
Caster sugar to taste
Juice of half an orange
2–3 tablespoons cherry wine

Stone the cherries and chop them into quarters, making sure that you save the juices that come from the fruits during this process. (Retain just a few cherries for final garnish.) Whip the cream until it becomes thick and add the juice of half an orange and a tablespoon of sugar. Whip again, adding the juices you have saved from the cherries and a little of the cherry wine. Whip again, and taste. You are aiming for a creamy mix which has taken as much wine as possible without losing its shape. Add cherries and mix well in.

Chill and serve in individual glass dishes. Top off each dish with cherries, squeezing them as you place them onto the dish so that their rich red juice pours down the side of the cream and adds extra colour.

Serve this dish with sweet biscuits on a fine summer's evening.

CRAB-APPLE

Crab-apple Wine

This delicious and colourful country wine is best made in early October. Choose the rosiest crab-apples you can find.

> *3 lb crab-apples*
> *3 lb demerara sugar*
> *1 gallon water*
> *1 oz yeast*

Slice each crab-apple in two, pour over the boiling water and leave in a covered bucket for a week. Strain off the liquor onto the demerara sugar. Stir well when cool. Add the yeast, cover closely and leave for 6 days before turning all into your demijohn and proceeding as on page 4.

Crab-apple wine is best if kept for at least a year.

Pork with Oranges and Crab-apple Wine

1 lb lean pork free from fat and diced into 1-inch cubes
Juice of 2 oranges
Rind from oranges sliced like matchsticks
About ¼ pint crab-apple wine
8 oz crab-apples, halved and pipped but not skinned
2 tablespoons sunflower oil to fry pork cubes
Small amount of flour to dust pork cubes
2 tablespoons dry mustard powder
1 tablespoon granulated sugar
Freshly-ground black peppercorns and salt to season

Mix together the dry mustard, sugar and a tablespoon flour with freshly ground peppercorns and salt to season. Roll the pork cubes in this mix until completely covered. Heat the oil in shallow frying pan and add pork cubes when it has reached a good strong heat. Fry pork, continually turning to prevent the sugar from catching and burning.

When meat is crisp and brown add equal amounts of crab-apple wine and orange juice and allow to bubble for a few moments. Lower the heat and add crab-apples and orange rind, then simmer gently adding a little more wine if needed to thin down sauce. Adjust seasoning. Cook for at least 10 minutes or until the pork is cooked.

Serve with a selection of green vegetables and boiled new potatoes if available, or if you wish plain boiled rice, which actually goes very well with this dish.

Several years ago a very special friend struggled through my cottage gate carrying a small crab-apple tree as a gift. 'I hope this brings you joy,' she said as she placed it at my front door. It has. Every spring its blossom increases in volume and it is now quite a spectacular sight, both during the blossom period and then throughout the summer as its fruit develops. By the time autumn has arrived it is usually groaning with fruit, much of which I use to make wine, though I do keep a little back to cook with and produce crab-apple jelly. I feel so sad when I see other crab-apple trees ignored when the fruit is ripe. Perhaps this recipe and Mollie's wine recipe will encourage people with these trees to fill their larders with the fruits rather than letting them rot on the ground.

DAMSON

Damson Wine

There don't seem to be many damson trees about in my area, but one old fellow I know always let me have some – providing I give him a bottle from the year before.

Damson wine is best made in late August or September.

> *4 lb damsons (ripe but firm)*
> *1 gallon water*
> *3 lb sugar*
> *1 oz yeast*
> *1 wineglass of brandy*

Wipe the damsons clean, take off any stalks and place the unstoned fruit in your container. Pour a gallon of boiling water over the fruit and bruise the damsons well by pressing them against the side of the container with a large wooden spoon. Cover the wine with a thick cloth and leave for 4 days, stirring well once a day. Strain through your muslin, gently squeezing out all the liquid. Tip in the sugar and stir well until all has dissolved, and add the yeast. Cover again and leave for a further 4 days. Strain off into the demijohn and fix the airlock. When it is time to bottle this off, top each bottle with a little brandy, using a wineglassful between all your bottles.

Cork well and leave if possible for at least a year, when it will look and taste almost like port.

Duckling with Damsons

4 duckling breasts or portions
¼ pint damson wine
1 lb damsons, stoned
2 tablespoons honey
2 tablespoons soy sauce
2 cloves garlic, crushed or chopped very fine
1 teaspoon arrowroot
Freshly ground black peppercorns and salt to season

Place the duckling portions on a rack which fits comfortably over a roasting tin (this is to catch the juices while allowing the heat to each part of the meat at once). Season the duck well and rub garlic into skin. Put the soy sauce and the honey into a jam jar or small container with a top and shake the ingredients together until you have a good mix. Then, using a pastry brush, paint the mix evenly over the duck portions. Bake in a moderate oven for about an hour, continually basting with the soy and honey mix until the duck is golden brown and cooked through.

While the duckling portions are cooking, make the sauce by poaching the fruit in the damson wine until the fruit is soft but still retains its shape. Strain the fruit and set aside in a warm place while you return the wine to the saucepan and bring it to the boil, reducing it by at least a third through rapid boiling. Pour into the reduced wine any honey-and-soy mix you have left, and add the juices from the bottom of the tray over which the duck are cooking – be careful to remove any fat as you do so. Thicken this liquid by adding the arrowroot which has been diluted with a little wine. Stir continually as the sauce cooks and thickens.

When duck portions are cooked, drain off the last drops of juice into the sauce and adjust seasoning. Pour sauce onto each individual plate so it completely covers the bottom. Place duck on top and garnish with cooked damsons.

DANDELION

Two Dandelion Wines

There is no excuse for anyone to say that they cannot find dandelions, but try not to pick them from the sides of a busy road. You will find dandelions blooming profusely from April through until June. The flowers must be freshly picked on a nice warm day.

(1)

This is one of the finest tonic wines, very good for those with a sluggish liver or indigestion. You will need quite a lot of dandelion *heads* for this, as it is wise to remove the little green collar round the flower head for this particular recipe.

> *3 quarts dandelion heads (pressed down firmly in a jug)*
> *1 gallon water*
> *3 lb sugar*
> *3 oranges*
> *1 oz yeast*

Hold the dandelion head upside down, cut off the green part, and put the petals into your bucket. Pour a gallon of boiling water over them. Cover with a cloth and leave for 2 days. Then tip all this into a large saucepan, add the grated orange rind, bring to the boil and boil steadily for 10 minutes. Cool a little and then strain into your bucket and add the sugar, stirring until it has dissolved. Add the juice from the oranges. When the wine is cooled add the yeast. Leave in the bucket, covered with a cloth, for 4 days. Then strain off into demijohn and fit the airlock. Bottle off when the wine has stopped working.

As well as being a 'tonic', this makes a very nice dinner wine.

St George's Day – 23 April – is considered to be the best day for picking dandelions (provided it's not raining!).

This makes a lovely golden-coloured wine, suitable for drinking at any time, with or without meals. Dandelion wine usually turns out sweet or semi-sweet.

(2)

This recipe does not involve removing the little green frill from the back of the flower head. Nonetheless, there must be *no* green stalks left on – otherwise the wine will have a very bitter taste.

> *3 quarts dandelion heads*
> *4 lb sugar*
> *2 lemons*
> *1 orange*
> *1 gallon water*
> *1 oz yeast*

Put the flower heads into your wine-making container and pour over them a gallon of boiling water. Cover closely and leave for 3 days, stirring each day. Then strain through your muslin. Pour into a large saucepan, and add the sugar and the grated rinds of the fruit. Bring up to the boil, simmer gently for about 20 minutes, then leave to cool a little. Put all this back into your bucket and add the juice of the fruit. When the wine is cool but not cold sprinkle on the yeast. Cover again and leave for a further 5 days. Strain and pour into your demijohn and continue as on page 4.

This is drinkable at any time after 6 months, but try leaving it for a year.

A townswoman who had recently come to live in the country was very keen to start making wine, like her country neighbours. One of them had said to her, 'Thurs plenty of dandelions about Missus, why don't you start with them?' The woman had noticed, when she came home on the bus, that just outside the village there was a field absolutely smothered with the bright yellow flowers. She planned that when her husband came home from work she would suggest that, after he'd had his tea, they should go along to the field to gather some.

The next morning she told her neighbour what happened. 'Well,' she said, 'last evening my Harry said that he'd come along with me, I was a bit nervous of going on me own, you see. We gets to the field and stood by the gate looking over. There wasn't a dandelion to be seen. Oh, he did go on – "Dragging me down here on a fool's errand after I've been hard at work all day," he said. I felt awful. So I shan't be able to make any dandelion wine now 'cos I don't know where to find any more.' Her neighbour started laughing.

''Tis no laughing matter,' the townswoman said. 'I did so want to be like you.'

'Look,' replied her country neighbour, 'you get your basket, we'll go down to that field and get you some dandelions.'

'But there ain't none there,' she replied.

''Course there is, them flowers, like a lot of others, "goes to sleep" come evening time, they'll all be out full again this morning now the sun's come out.'

Beautiful, bountiful summer harvest:
first make your wines – and then cook with them

Combining the first roses of the year with tasty trout (page 140)

*The heady perfume of elderflowers enhances
both wine and fritters (page 70)*

Four stages of blackberry wine – Mollie's favourite tipple (page 30)

*Elderberries produce a robust wine which enhances this delicious
beef hot pot, a winter warmer (page 60)*

*The delicate perfume of honeysuckle wine blends beautifully with
the fruits of summer (page 83)*

Dandelions – picked and drunk on St George's Day (page 52)

Beetroot wine, brown bread and bortsch – a meal in itself (page 27)

*Using sage to bring out the flavours – pork chops with sage wine
sauce (page 147)*

Rabbit Casserole in Dandelion Wine

*2 rabbits, if they are small (rabbits vary a great deal in size
— you alone will know just how much meat you need to
satisfy your family)*
1 pint dandelion wine
2 dessertspoons sunflower oil to fry rabbit portions
Flour to dust rabbits
1 bunch spring onions, chopped roughly
Handful parsley, chopped fine
*Cup of dandelion heads picked from an area away from the
main road*
10 succulent fresh inner leaves from the dandelion plant
*Bunch of baby carrots if available, left whole (if using old
carrots, chop roughly)*
1 green pepper, sliced roughly
1 bay leaf
Freshly ground black peppercorns and salt to season

Portion rabbit and wash thoroughly before dusting with seasoned
flour. Fry off rabbit portions, turning to brown on all sides. Place
rabbit in casserole dish when brown but not completely cooked.

In the remaining juices gently fry all vegetables and herbs,
leaving the dandelion leaves and flowers to one side for a moment.
To this mix add the wine and allow to bubble for a moment before
seasoning the sauce. Pour the mix over the rabbit portions. Add to
the casserole dish the petals from the dandelion heads and the
dandelion leaves which have been roughly chopped. Stir in so that
they are covered with the sauce.

Cook in a moderate oven for at least $1\frac{1}{2}$ hours or until the
rabbit flesh begins to fall off the bone. Taste and adjust seasoning
if necessary. Decorate with a very few uncooked dandelion petals
to add a subtle flourish of colour.

Serve with simple garden vegetables and crusty bread to mop
up the juices.

Christmas 1910

The Wilks family – nine of them – were very much looking forward
to their Christmas dinner. They were going to have a joint of
beef, which was very unusual for them, more often it was a
couple of rabbits or one of their own cockerels. A joint of beef was
unheard of in their home – after all Mr Wilks was just a carter on
the local estate and his wages were only £1 a week. But
Mrs Wilks had been paying tuppence a week on a card at the
butcher's, so she chose a rib-of-beef joint. The smell of that meat
roasting in the old fire oven was unbelievable. In the
big tin along with the meat were two or three pounds of potatoes, all
covered in dripping. When the potatoes were done, Mrs Wilks took
them out of the meat tin and put them in another to keep warm.
Then she poured the Yorkshire pudding mixture all round the meat. In
about twenty minutes time the dinner would be ready. Mr Wilks, back
from seeing to his horses, said that he would carve the joint.
'Missus,' he said, 'fetch I that bone handle carving knife.' The knife
which had not been used for ages was brought.
'Coo', he said, 'he's as blunt as old 'Arry, I shall have to pop up to
the farm and sharpen him on the grinston (grindstone).' The farm
was only a little way from their cottage.
'Well, dun't be long, the dinner's nearly ready,' Mrs Wilks called after
him, as she pushed the boiling Brussels back down into the water.
The children were beside themselves – what a dinner they were going
to have. They were already sitting up to the table, knives
and forks at the ready.
'Wherevers that man got to!,' Mrs Wilks remarked for the hundredth
time. It was now nearly three o'clock, and the meat and potatoes
had been in and out that old fire many times. The Brussels – strained
up ages ago – had taken on a dark greeny-brown look,
and the Yorkshire pudding, which had raised up that much it had
nearly touched the oven roof, was now looking brown, hard
and flat. They were all so hungry and tired of waiting. At four
o'clock, Mrs Wilks said, 'I think we'll have ours.'
She dished up the meal, the longed-for beef was so hard that
Mrs Wilks couldn't cut it properly with an ordinary knife, so they had

to have lumps rather than slices, and everything else was overdone.
But they were all so hungry that the plates were soon cleared,
and then they had Christmas pudding which they all enjoyed
with lashings of custard on.
At half-past four they heard the sound of someone playing
a mouth organ.
'I'll bet that's him!' Mrs Wilks cried, 'He always plays that
damned thing when he's drunk.'
The music stopped and Mr Wilks, red-faced and grinning
like a Cheshire cat, opened the door, and stood there leaning
against it.
'My blessed,' he said, slurring his words, 'that dandelion
wine of Gaffer's is some strong stuff.'
'Never mind that,' his wife replied, 'where's the carving knife?'
'What carving knife?' he said.
'The one you took up to the farmhouse hours and hours ago,
to sharpen it, you said, so as you could carve our Christmas beef.'
'Oh, ah,' he replied, still grinning, 'so I did. Well, what
about a bit of Christmas dinner, then, mother?'
'There's none for you,' she cried, 'we had ours ages ago, spoilt
it was while we was waiting for you, and you can go and sleep in the
henhouse,' and she slammed the door in his face.
Joe Wilks stumbled down the garden path, playing 'Felix
Kept on Walking' on his mouth organ. Then he fell, dead-drunk, in
the henhouse where he stayed until it was time to go to
work the next morning.

ELDERBERRY

Two Elderberry Wines

Every autumn the elderberries hang purply-black from the bushes in my area. I feel I would like to use them all but, of course, that is impossible. However, I do manage to make about 4 gallons of wine. Late September and early October is the best time to pick elderberries.

(1)

> *3 lb elderberries (after removing the stalks)*
> *3 lb sugar*
> *1 gallon water*
> *1 lemon*
> *½ oz yeast*
> *1 lb raisins (for a sweeter wine)*
> *1 lb damsons or blackberries (optional)*

Pick your berries on a warm balmy autumn day – you can tell that they are truly ripe when the birds begin to eat them. To remove the berries frm the stalks use the prongs of a table fork. Weigh them, put them into your bucket, pour on the gallon of boiling water and mash the berries against the side of the container with a large wooden spoon. Cover and leave for 3 or 4 days. Strain and tip the liquid back into your clean bucket, add the sugar and stir till you think it has all dissolved. Squeeze the lemon and add all the juice. Sprinkle on the yeast. Cover for 3 days, strain again and pour the wine into your demijohn, fix the airlock and continue as on page 4.

This will produce a medium-dry wine, rich and full-bodied. Should you wish to make a sweeter wine, just add 1 lb of raisins, split and chopped, when you add the boiling water at the beginning of the recipe.

You can also add 1 lb of damsons or blackberries to this wine, at the same time as you add the elderberries. When this has matured it will taste almost like burgundy.

You can dry elderberries in the sun and then make a good nonalcoholic drink in wintertime by pouring water on them and adding sugar to taste. Excellent for a head cold.

(2)

This wine will have a rich spicy taste, and is excellent when mulled as a winter drink. Taken hot at bedtime it will induce sleep, and also help to sweat out a cold. And, of course, it makes a lovely rich red wine suitable for drinking with most meaty meals.

> *3 lb 8 oz elderberries*
> *3 lb demerara sugar*
> *1 lb raisins*
> *½ oz ground ginger*
> *1 teaspoon cinnamon*
> *4 cloves*
> *½ oz root ginger (bruised)*
> *1 lemon*
> *1 gallon water*
> *½ oz yeast*

Strip the berries from the stalks, and weigh them. Put them into your bucket and pour the gallon of boiling water over them. Cover and let them stand for 24 hours. Bruise them well with a wooden spoon before straining them off. Measure the liquid, and to every gallon add the 3 lb of sugar and thinly sliced lemon. Now boil up the cloves, raisins, cinnamon and the two lots of ginger in a little of the wine. Strain this and tip into the wine. Sprinkle on the yeast. Cover with a thick cloth and leave for 4 days. Strain and pour the wine into the demijohn, fix the airlock and continue as on page 4. The wine is drinkable within 4 months.

There is a lot of goodness in elderberries. One old herbalist reckoned that the elder tree was God's most valuable gift to mankind.

Elderberry Beef Pot with Elderberry Wine

1 lb good quality braising steak, chopped into 1 inch cubes
2 medium onions, chopped fine
8 oz mushrooms, chopped fine
2 oz tomato paste
1 lb fresh tomatoes, chopped fine
½ pint elderberry wine
½ pint good brown stock (if you use a stock cube, reduce the
    salt when you season)
2 cloves garlic, chopped very fine
Bunch parsley, chopped fine
2 sprigs marjoram, chopped fine
2 sprigs thyme, chopped fine
1 bay leaf
Flour to dust beef
3 teaspoons sunflower oil to fry.
Handful fresh elderberries (these freeze very well so don't
    be ashamed of using frozen elderberries)
Freshly ground black peppercorns and salt to season

Trim all the fat off the beef and cut into 1 inch cubes. Prepare herbs and vegetables. Heat the sunflower oil in large frying pan and fry off the beef cubes which have been dusted with flour and seasoned. Fry at good heat until the chunks of beef are well browned and sealed. Add to the pan the onions, mushrooms, garlic and fry for long enough to cook the onions and mush-rooms. Add tomatoes, tomato paste and herbs and stir the mix well. Sprinkle a little flour onto the meat and vegetables and cook in for a moment. Add the elderberry wine and let the mix sizzle – stir all the time. Thin down with a little stock or water until you have a fine sauce. Season and add a small handful of elderberries (reserving just a few for the final garnish).

Pour the mixture into a good-sized casserole dish and cook for at least 1½ hours in a slow-to-medium oven, or until the meat is tender. You will notice at this stage that you have a very rich, almost black sauce; this is from the elderberry juice and makes a fine contrast when served against mashed potatoes or white vegetables. Adjust seasoning before serving and at the last moment toss in a few more elderberries.

Serve this dish on a bitterly cold day when you need something warm and filling to keep out the chill.

Jugged Hare with Elderberry Wine

1 hare which has been hung for at least 4 days
1 onion studded with 6 cloves
1 bunch parsley, chopped fine
4 sprigs thyme, chopped fine
2 sprigs of marjoram, chopped fine
¼ pint elderberry wine
1 teaspoon vinegar
*1 pint good rich brown stock (if you use a stock cube, reduce
    the salt content when seasoning)*
2 tablespoons redcurrant jelly
Flour to dust hare
3 tablespoons sunflower oil to fry hare
Pinch powdered mace
Pinch nutmeg
Freshly ground black peppercorns and salt to season

Skin the hare and joint, reserving all blood and the liver. Mix the blood with the vinegar (this prevents it curdling during the cooking process) and keep cool until needed. Dust the joints of meat with seasoned flour and fry in the oil until all sides are golden brown. Place in large casserole and cover with stock, onion, herbs, mace and nutmeg. Season this mix and cook for at least 2½ hours in a moderate oven of 350 °F.

When the hare is cooked take out the meat and keep warm and strain the liquor into a large saucepan and bring to the boil. Add the redcurrant jelly and slowly and carefully pour the blood into the mix, stirring all the time. Do not boil the liquid at this stage as you will spoil the whole dish. Add the elderberry wine and adjust the seasoning. Serve either by pouring the sauce over the joints of hare on a serving dish, or by returning the whole lot to a casserole dish.

Traditionally jugged hare has been garnished with shaped fried-bread snippets which are usually placed on the outer edge of the serving dish.

Elderberry Wine Pâté

◇◇◇

1 clove garlic
4 tablespoons elderberry wine
1 oz elderberries (these can be frozen – they freeze very
*   well and make a useful standby ingredient if you are*
*   looking for flavour and colour)*
8 oz minced pork
8 oz minced chicken breasts
4 oz minced pork fat
2 tablespoons sunflower oil
4 oz mushrooms, diced small
1 medium onion, diced very fine
4 sprigs thyme, chopped fine
2 sprigs marjoram, chopped fine
4 sprigs parsley, chopped fine
Pinch ground nutmeg
1 egg, beaten well
6 (approximately – depending on width) slices streaky
*   bacon to line pâté tin*
Freshly ground black peppercorns and salt to season

Heat the oil in a reasonably large saucepan and gently fry off the diced mushrooms, onions and garlic until soft cooked but not brown. Add elderberry wine, thyme, marjoram, parsley and nutmeg, bring to the boil for a moment and then reduce heat, cover the pan and allow to simmer for 5 minutes. Remove the saucepan from the heat and add minced pork, pork fat and chicken. Stir well and then add herbs and egg and mix again until all the ingredients are mixed well together. Adjust seasoning.

Line a pound loaf tin with streaky bacon slices, covering the sides and the bottom of tin. Pack in half the meat mix and then, after packing in firmly, scatter the elderberries onto the surface and over with the remaining meat mix. Place the pâté tin in a large flat roasting tray filled with water (this will reduce the speed of cooking and prevent the sides from burning before the rest is done). Place the tray gently (easy to cover the kitchen floor with water at this stage!) into the oven and cook at about 350 °F for 1¼ hours.

Remove from the oven. You will find that there is a residue of elderberry wine liquid which has separated from the dish. When it is cool enough, carefully pour it out and set to one side. Chill the pâté until needed.

The elderberry liquid should have become a reasonably firm jelly when cooled – sufficient to serve as a jellied sauce side dish. (I frequently place this in a bowl and arrange pâté slices around it for an attractive finish.) However, I have also heated the residue, and after thickening it with a little cornflour or arrowroot, served it as a hot sauce. Either way, you will find it is a very flavoursome sauce which has picked up both the meat flavours and the herbs too.

Braised Rabbit with Elderberry Wine

2 small rabbits or 1 large one (size depends on appetites)
2 medium onions, chopped fine
4 Jerusalem artichokes, sliced
1 large cooking apple, diced roughly
4 oz grapes (any colour), seeds removed
4 oz mushrooms, chopped roughly
4 oz carrots, chopped roughly
1 bunch mixed herbs including parsley, thyme and marjoram,
*   chopped fine*
2 oz raisins, seeded
Flour to dust rabbit portions
3 tablespoons sunflower oil
½ pint elderberry wine
Rind from 1 orange, grated or cut into matchstick-shaped strips
1 clove garlic, chopped very fine
¼ pint good rich brown stock (remember if you cheat and use
*   a stock cube, do reduce the salt when you season the dish)*
Freshly ground black peppercorns and salt to season

Prepare rabbit by jointing and removing as many bones as possible. Wash well and dust with seasoned flour. Fry rabbit portions in sunflower oil until golden brown but not cooked through, then place in a casserole dish.

In the remaining oil and juices fry the artichokes until almost soft, then add onions, mushrooms, carrots, herbs and garlic. Pour on the wine and allow the liquid to bubble a few moments before adding the stock and adjusting the seasoning. Pour the sauce over the rabbit joints, adding the grapes, orange rind, chopped apple and raisins. Cook for at least 3 hours in a slow-to-moderate oven.

The addition of grapes, orange rind, apples and raisins to this dish will provide a sweet yet tangy flavour which is both rich and tasty. Because of the strength of the final flavour I find it best to serve this dish with very simple vegetables as an accompaniment – so that there is no clash of flavours.

Spiced Apple and Elderberry Tart

For the pastry
4 oz margarine
8 oz wholemeal flour
A little water

For the filling
4 large cooking apples, peeled and sliced
1 cup elderberries, fresh or frozen
Generous amount elderberry wine
1 cinnamon stick, 6 cloves and a few allspice tied in a muslin
  bag
Sugar to sweeten apples, amount depending on taste
1–2 teaspoons arrowroot
1 egg for egg wash (milk will do if you can't spare an egg)

Make up pastry in usual way and allow to rest in cool place while you prepare filling. Heat elderberry wine and spices together in pan until the flavours are well infused, then remove spices. When the wine has taken on a nice spicy flavour add the apples and elderberries and poach until fruit is tender. Sugar can be added to this mix if needed. Strain contents and retain the juices. Allow filling to cool a little, then prepare pastry for tart.

Roll out half the pastry and line your dish (8-inch dish suitable). Spoon in filling. Roll out remaining pastry for lid, decorate if you wish. Place in a preheated moderate oven for 20 to 30 minutes or until the pastry is golden brown.

Reduce the juices you strained off earlier by placing in a pan and allowing to bubble for a few moments. To this add the arrowroot diluted in a little elderberry wine and stir well until mixture thickens. Sweeten if required – normally the wine is sweet enough, but you may require more. Serve pie and sauce while hot for best effect.

Slithering Chitterlings

Owen Richards had a little farm on one side of a mountain in Wales, and his friend and nearest neighbour, Alan Lewis, had one on the other side about three miles away. And when it was pig-killing time they always helped each other out. On this particular day, Alan was having his pigs killed so Owen set off early that morning to give him a hand.

'Take a bucket for the chitlins,' his wife called – she knew Alan would give them to him for helping out. 'And don't get drinking too much of their home-made wine – their elderberry's lethal.'

It was hours and hours later when Owen's wife heard someone singing 'Land of My Fathers', away in the distance.

'That's him for a crown,' she said. And some while later, a very wet but happy Owen stumbled into the kitchen with the empty bucket on his arm.

'You're drunk,' she screamed, 'and where's the chitlins?'

'They're flowing down the mountain stream,' he replied.

'What 'du mean flowing down the mountain stream? They would have lasted us for two or three days for our supper.'

'Well,' he went on, slurring his words, 'you know we've had a tidy drop of rain lately, and that old mountain stream was running like Niagara. I got half way across, and stumbled over a boulder and fell flat on me face. But I kept hold of the bucket, knowing how you looks for the chitlins. But the bucket just filled up with water and then them chitlins just slithered out of the bucket and into the stream, and they went tumbling over the stones, sliding and slithering along till they were out of sight.'

ELDERFLOWER

Two Elderflower Wines

(1)

This is best made in May and June, when the creamy flowers of the elder grow almost everywhere in the country.

> *2 pints elderflower*
> *3 lb sugar*
> *2 lemons*
> *1 gallon water*
> *½ oz yeast*

Be sure that it's a nice dry sunny day when you go out to gather your elderflowers. When you pick them, always give them a little shake, and if the petals fall, don't use them, otherwise the wine will taste how elderflowers smell which is quite unpleasant. Put the elder florets into your wine-making bucket, with no bits of green on them at all. Add the grated rind of the lemons and the sugar, and pour over them a gallon of boiling water. Stir well and leave to cool. Add the lemon juice, and the yeast, cover with a cloth and leave for 3 days. Strain, then tip into the demijohn, fix the airlock and proceed as on page 4.

This will make a delicate light amber-coloured sweet wine, drinkable after 6 months.

(2)

This is also best made in May and June.

2 pints elderflower heads
1 lb raisins (the ones with pips in if possible)
Juice of a large grapefruit
3 lb sugar
White of 1 egg
1 gallon water
1 oz yeast

Tip the sugar into a large saucepan, add the water and stir well. Beat up the white of egg and add, again stirring well. Boil for about 25 minutes. Take off from the heat and at once skim off any scum that has risen. Pick over the elderflowers so that no green at all remains, then put them into your bucket. Add the grapefruit juice, and the raisins, each one should be split open with the thumbs), then pour in the warm liquid from the saucepan. When this has cooled down add the yeast. Cover the wine and leave in the bucket for the next 4 days, stirring it daily. Strain again into the demijohn and fix the airlock. Leave for at least a month before either bottling off or putting into a cask or stone jar.

A delicate sweet pale amber-coloured wine, it should be ready to drink in 6 months.

Elderflower Fritters with Gooseberry Sauce

For the fritters
8 sprigs elderflowers, picked when they have just left the
bud stage
6 tablespoons elderflower wine
3 oz wholewheat flour
2 eggs, beaten
1 tablespoon sunflower oil for batter
Sunflower oil to fry fritters

For the sauce
1 lb gooseberries
¼ pint elderflower wine
2 sprigs elderflower
Sugar to taste, the amount will depend on the fruit's sweetness
Caster sugar to dust finished fritters

Prepare the batter by adding eggs to the flour and beating well. Add to the flour and eggs the tablespoon of sunflower oil and the 6 tablespoons of elderflower wine. Beat the mixture very well and leave to stand for at least half an hour in a cool place. Prepare the sauce by putting the gooseberries, wine, elderflowers and a little sugar together in a saucepan and allowing to simmer gently over a low heat until the fruit is completely cooked. Remove the 2 elderflower heads when the mix is cooked and cool enough to extract them, then put the cool mix into a blender or pass through a sieve – you are aiming for a reasonably thick purée. Adjust the flavour of sauce by adding a little more sugar at this stage if needed.

Prepare to cook the fritters by dipping the elderflower heads into the batter one at a time, holding them by the stem and allowing excess batter to drip away before frying them in a deep pan of hot oil that has been heated to at least 325 °F. Fry the elderflowers in batches, as they will be inclined to stick together if there are too many in the pan at the same time. Drain the fritters on kitchen paper and dust with caster sugar. Serve with the gooseberry purée while they are still warm.

GOOSEBERRY

Gooseberry Wine

I like to use really ripe gooseberries to make my wine in May–July, though some folk prefer them to be hard and green. You will need

> *4 lb gooseberries*
> *3 lb sugar*
> *1 gallon water*
> *½ oz yeast*

Top and tail the gooseberries and put them into your bucket. Pour over the boiling water and bruise the gooseberries well with a large wooden spoon, or an old-fashioned wooden rolling pin, pressing them against the side of the bucket. Cover with a cloth and leave for a couple of days. Strain, squeezing out as much of the juice as possible. Now add the sugar and the yeast. Cover again and leave for 5 days. Strain again. Pour the wine into the demijohn, fix the airlock and leave to ferment in a warm room. Then bottle off.

Gooseberry wine is best left for at least a year. Sometimes it will turn into a sparkling wine by accident. So watch it after you have bottled it off, as sometimes a third fermentation will take place. If this happens, re-bottle it off into champagne-type bottles and lightly cork with plastic screw corks, which can be eased if necessary. The wine should then be stored on its side in a cool place.

A local farmer was given champagne at a party. When asked by his host how he liked his drink, he replied, 'Ah, 'tis a nice drop o'gooseberry wine, but it 'ent as good as my missus makes.'

Gooseberry wine is known as 'poor man's champagne'.

Deep Fried Camembert Cheese with Gooseberry Wine Sauce

1 round Camembert cheese weighing about 8 oz
1 fresh egg, beaten well
1 cupful fresh brown breadcrumbs
2 tablespoons of flour to dust Camembert portions
Enough sunflower oil to fill a deep fat frying pan
4 tablespoons home-made gooseberry jam
4 tablespoons gooseberry wine
8 fresh dessert gooseberries – if available – for garnish
Fresh lemon balm leaves – if available – for garnish

Cut the Camembert into 8 portions and dust with seasoned flour. Place the beaten egg into a shallow dish, and do the same with the breadcrumbs. Dip the floured cheese portions first into the egg and then the breadcrumbs, coating them evenly until there is no cheese showing through. Set aside the coated cheese in a cool place for at least half an hour.

Prepare the sauce by warming the jam and diluting with the wine. Do not boil or make too hot – you just need a warm sauce, not a hot one. When you need to serve the cheese portions, heat the oil until it reaches at least 350 °F and drop the cheese portions in one by one. Do not attempt to cook them in one batch – 4 at once is enough as they cook very quickly, but tend to stick together if too crowded. Drain on kitchen paper to remove any excess oil and serve at once while really hot, with the sauce as a side dip. Garnish with gooseberries and lemon balm.

This dish may sound ridiculous to those who have never tried frying Camembert, but be assured it makes a super starter to a meal, or a useful extra at a fingers-only party.

Gooseberry Fool with Gooseberry Wine Sauce

1 lb fresh gooseberries
2 elderflower heads
1 pint Jersey cream, whipped thick
Caster sugar to taste
1 or 2 drops edible green food dye
1 teaspoon arrowroot or cornflour to thicken sauce
¼ pint gooseberry wine

Place wine, gooseberries and elderflower heads together in a saucepan with a little sugar to taste and simmer gently until fruit is cooked and very soft. Strain off liquid and retain. Remove elderflower heads from gooseberries (they are not needed now they have done their job). When fruit is cool enough, mash or pulp in liquidizer until a soft purée is obtained, then set aside and chill.

With the liquid which was used to cook the fruit make a sauce by adidng a couple of drops of colouring. Be careful at this stage because too much colouring will make the dish look unappetizing; too little and you need not have bothered in the first place. Bring the coloured liquid to the boil and add arrowroot or cornflour that has been mixed with a small amount of gooseberry wine. Stir continuously while the arrowroot mix does its job of thickening the sauce. Remove from heat and chill.

Whip the cream and combine with the fruit purée. Spoon the fool into one large glass dish or separate dishes and then pour the sauce on top in great swirls so that it beats its way through into the fool and adds an attractive finish. If you wish, you can line the dishes with a little of the sauce before adding the fool, or you can add it to the fool before you serve it up. It is a matter of choice – all methods work and provide an attractive finish.

This is a real country dish – popular because of its simplicity and the honest early summer flavour that it produces.

GORSE

Gorse Wine

'Kissing's out of fashion when the gorse is not in bloom' – I don't know who first said it, but whoever did so was right, because on the commons you can always find a few flowers out, even in the dead of winter. However, September is perhaps the best time to make gorse wine.

Gorse wine is reputed to be excellent for the kidneys, and in my grandmother's day it was often given to people with the 'dropsy'; but it also makes a nice dinner wine. Mine always seems to turn out a little on the dry side (I prefer sweet or semi-sweet wines), so if you like your wine dry, try this one.

You will need gloves, a pair of scissors and an old clean white cotton pillowcase to drop the flowers into – if you do this carefully there will be no need to pick them over when you get home, and you can keep them in the pillowcase during the wine-making process. You will need

> *2 lb gorse flowers*
> *3 lb sugar*
> *2 lemons*
> *2 oranges*
> *1 gallon water*
> *½ oz yeast*

Keep the flowers in the bag or pillowcase and place them in a large saucepan. Boil half the water, pour it into the saucepan and simmer for about 15 minutes. Meanwhile boil up the rest of the water; tip this and the water from the saucepan into your wine-making container, after you have squeezed as much of the liquid as possible from the pillow case. Add the suger and the

grated rinds of both lemons and oranges; then add the juices from
the lemons and oranges, stir well and leave to cool. Add the yeast,
cover and leave for a week. Then strain and continue as directed
on page 4.

This is well worth the 'prickles' that you might have to put up
with when gathering the flowers. It is drinkable in 6 months, and
should be a rich golden colour.

Cod Fillets Poached in Gorse Wine

4 portions of fresh cod
A handful gorse flowers for decoration
½ pint gorse wine
1 lemon
1 handful parsley, chopped fine
1 bunch spring onions, chopped roughly
1 bay leaf
Freshly ground black peppercorns and salt to season

Season cod fillets and place in shallow pan. Cover them with the wine, using a little more than the recipe suggests if necessary. Add chopped spring onions, parsley and bay leaf and simmer gently with lid on pan for long enough for the fish to cook. This fish cooks quickly so beware of overcooking.

Remove the fish from the stock and keep warm while you reduce the stock by bringing it to a rapid boil for some moments. When the liquid is reduced by at least a third, add the juice of one lemon and adjust seasoning. Pour finished sauce over fish and garnish with a few gorse petals and parsley for extra effect.

Serve with mixed green salad into which you can toss a few gorse flowers.

GRAPEFRUIT

Grapefruit Wine

This is one of the simplest wines to make, although of course it is a little expensive.

> *8 grapefruit*
> *1 gallon water*
> *3 lb 8 oz sugar*
> *1 oz yeast*

Slice the grapefruit – don't peel them, but remove the pips – and put them in your bucket. Pour over them a gallon of cold water. Cover and leave for 5 days, stirring daily. Then strain and add the sugar and yeast. Cover again and leave for a couple of days. Pour into the demijohn and continue as directed on page 4.

This is a quick-maturing wine, and will be ready to drink in 4 months. It is considered to be a good tonic and 'pick-me-up' as well as a very pleasant dinner wine. This really tastes of grapefruit, and is a lovely golden colour.

Grilled Grapefruit with Grapefruit Wine

2 grapefruit
4 tablespoons brown sugar
A generous slurp or two of grapefruit wine
Fresh fruit to garnish – orange slices, blackberries and
*   raspberries make good contrast*

Cut grapefruit in half and prepare as you would for an ordinary breakfast dish by cutting each segment free with a grapefruit knife and removing pith from the centre. Place prepared fruit in a reasonably deep dish and pour a generous amount of wine into the centre of each, till it overflows into the dish. Sprinkle 1 dessertspoon brown sugar onto each fruit. Arrange garnish according to taste, or not if you like things to stand alone. Bake in a moderate oven until sugar has begun to melt and brown the fruit and a nice sticky sauce is developing in the cooking dish. Serve hot with the extra juices from the tray poured over the finished dish.

The beauty of this dish is that it can be prepared in advance and popped into the oven just 15 minutes before you need it to start the meal. It stimulates the appetite and acts as a nice warming start to a meal on a cold winter's day. Besides which, it looks terrific and the added flavour of the wine brings out the full grapefruit taste.

Orange and Grapefruit Cocktail

2 large grapefruit
4 oranges
Caster sugar to taste
Grapefruit wine (with this recipe it really is a case of just
*   slurping it on until you think you have added enough)*

(Note that you could also make this dish with orange wine.)

Remove the segments of grapefruit and orange and keep whole, making sure that as much pith as possible has been cleaned away from the fruit. Chill four glasses while preparing this dish, frosting the rims with sugar is desired. (This is done by simply rubbing an orange segment round the rim of the glass and then inserting the glass into a shallow dish of sugar to create the frosted-rim effect.) To the segments of fruit add a little sugar to sweeten (if necessary) and enough wine to create a good sauce.

Allow the fruit to mix with the wine for at least a couple of hours or more if possible, for the longer they are allowed to stand the better the flavour. Spoon segments and juice into frosted glasses and serve as a first course or as a refreshing dessert.

I do not serve cream or anything else with this dish – I find cream does nothing to enhance its flavours as it does with other fruit-based dishes.

GREENGAGE

Greengage Wine

Late July and early August is the right time to make this, and just every so often we have a bumper crop of greengages. You will need

> 4 lb ripe greengages
> 1 gallon water
> 3 lb sugar
> ½ oz yeast
> gin

Halve the fruit, taking out the stones, and put the fleshy gages into your bucket. Pour over the boiling water. Cover and leave for five days. Strain off, adding the sugar, and stir well. Add the yeast to the liquid. Cover again and leave for at least a week. Strain, pour into the demijohn, fix the airlock, let the wine ferment, and proceed as on page 4. Bottle off in the usual way, adding a tablespoon of gin to each bottle.

The wine should be ready to drink in six months. If you prefer a not-too-sweet wine, cut down the amount of sugar to 2 lb 8 oz.

Greengage Crumble with Greengage Wine

1 lb greengages
4 oz sugar to cook fruit
½ pint greengage wine
2 oz brown sugar to make crumble mix
6 oz wholemeal flour
2 oz sesame seeds
2 oz sunflower seeds
2 oz butter
2 oz walnuts, chopped fine

Place greengages in pie dish along with sugar to sweeten. (Sugar may not be needed if the greengages are very ripe.) Pour wine over the fruit and leave for a moment while you prepare the crumble. Mix together the flour, sesame seeds, sunflower seeds, walnuts, butter and brown sugar until the mixture resembles breadcrumbs. Spoon the crumble mixture onto the fruit. Cook in a moderate oven until the fruit is cooked and the crumble topping is golden brown. Serve with fresh Jersey cream or yoghurt.

HONEYSUCKLE

Honeysuckle Wine

2 pints honeysuckle flowers
2 lemons
2 sticks rhubarb, roughly chopped
3 lb sugar
1 oz yeast
1 gallon water

Make sure you pick the flowers on a nice sunny morning while the dew is still on them. Place the flower heads and rhubarb into your wine-making bucket and pour on 1 gallon of boiling water. Add the juice from the 2 lemons and the sugar. Stir this well and cover until it has cooled enough to add the yeast (if you add the yeast while the mixture is too hot, it won't work). Stir the mixture twice a day for at least 5 days. Strain into your demijohn and proceed as on page 4.

This is a very delicate wine which usually turns out to have a beautiful pale-pink finish. You can almost smell the summer as you pour it into the glass 6 months later.

Mixed Summer Fruit Flan with a Honeysuckle Wine Glaze

◇◇◇

*Enough shortcrust pastry to line a shallow flan dish
(usually 4 oz flour and 2 oz margarine makes more than
enough)*
1 oz sesame seeds to add to the pastry for a nutty finish
1 teaspoon granulated sugar to add to the pastry
*A mix of summer fruits including cherries, raspberries,
gooseberries, strawberries and redcurrants if possible*
4 tablespoons honeysuckle wine
½ pint Jersey cream
1–2 teaspoons cornflour or arrowroot to thicken glaze

Make up pastry, adding sesame seeds and sugar to the mix before
you finish off with the water. Line flan dish with pastry and bake
blind in a moderate oven. Take care to prick the base of the pastry
with a fork to prevent it rising during the cooking process. When
flan case is cooked, whip cream, add a small amount of honeysuckle wine and whip again. (One tablespoonful should be enough
to colour and flavour the cream.) Fill the flan case with cream,
spreading it evenly all over the base.

Using your imagination, add the mixed fruits. I usually start
with a ring of redcurrants on the outer rim to define the edge, then
work inwards using the colours I have available to determine the
circular pattern – you are aiming to cover the cream completely
and produce a rainbow effect with the fruits. Heat the remaining
wine and thicken with arrowroot or cornflour, which has been
diluted in a little wine, and then added to the bubbling liquid until
a reasonably thick (but not too thick) sauce has been achieved.
When it is cool enough, use a pastry brush to paint the glaze onto
the finished flan, being careful not to be too heavy handed for it's
easy to get carried away and completely cover the fruit, so that all
you see is a layer of glaze.

LAST OF THE SUMMER FRUITS

Last of the Summer Fruits Wine

I made this one in August. It is a brand-new recipe which I created last summer. This is what I used:

> *1 lb early blackberries*
> *1 lb early Victoria plums*
> *1 lb sweet-scented rose petals*
> *3 lb sugar*
> *1 lemon*
> *1 orange*
> *1 gallon water*
> *$\frac{1}{2}$ oz yeast*

Take the stones from the plums and roll the blackberries in a cloth to clean them. Then place the rose petals, blackberries and plums into your wine-making bucket and pour over a gallon of boiling water. Cover with a thick cloth and leave for 3 days, stirring two or three times a day. Strain and squeeze out as much liquid as possible. Pour this liquid into your bucket and tip in the sugar, the juice and the rinds of both the lemon and orange, stir well until the sugar has dissolved and then sprinkle on the yeast. Cover well and stand the bucket in a warm place. Leave for a week, then strain again and pour the wine into your demijohn. Proceed as on page 4.

This makes a delicate sweet wine with a slightly scented bouquet; it's a lovely pinky-red in colour. Drinkable after 4 months – just right for Christmas in fact – its taste will bring a breath of summer into the dark days of winter.

Summer Pudding with the Last of the Summer Fruits Wine

Enough white bread to line a pound pudding basin
Butter to grease the basin
1 lb mixed berry fruits including redcurrants, blackcurrants, raspberries, tayberries and strawberries if possible (I find a dominance of redcurrants really brings out the summer flavour)
Sugar to sweeten fruit, amount will depend on the quality and sweetness of fruit
¼ pint wine

Cut the crusts from the bread slices and halve each slice. Grease the pudding basin with butter. Carefully place the slices of bread around the inside of the basin, so that they overlap slightly to form a perfect case for the fruit. Keep enough bread back to cover the top later. Place all the fruit, sugar to taste, and wine into a large saucepan and gently poach the fruit until it is cooked but not overdone. Try to keep some of the red- and blackcurrants whole if possible. Spoon the cooked fruit into the basin, and press down firmly. When completely full, line top with remaining bread slices and press again. Pour remaining juices over the top.

Cover with a saucer which has been weighed down with a heavy object – a 2 lb weight is perfect. Try to allow the pudding to stand weighed down for at least 12 hours, keeping it all the while in a cool place. Allow it to reach room temperature before serving as the fruits will give off more of their flavour this way. When ready to serve, turn out onto a large dish which is deep enough to catch any juices which may escape when the pudding is sliced. Enjoy with generous servings of thick Jersey cream or yoghurt.

Mollie and I usually freeze enough summer fruits to make this dish up at Christmastime. It makes a special treat after all the rich puddings and preserved fruits.

Fresh Fruit Salad Using the Last of the Summer Fruits Wine

*Gather together all the fruits you can find, remembering to
balance flavour and colour as you do so
A generous amount of last of the summer fruits wine*

Simply decide on a shape that will suit all the fruits that you have
acquired and dice apples, pears or peaches to match the smallest
fruit you have, or be adventurous and allow each of the fruits to
dictate the shape you should slice, dice or cut it into – some are
best left just as they are. Fill a large and attractive glass dish with
the fruit and pour on a generous quantity of wine. Stir in the wine
and serve after the fruit salad has been chilled for an hour or so.
(By letting it stand for a while you are allowing the fruits to pick
up the flavour of the wine and thus improving the dish.) Serve
with fresh yoghurt or rich thick Jersey cream and sweet biscuits.
Garnish with mint or lemon balm, borage or pineapple sage.

MANGOLD

Mangold Wine

It's a bit of a job to get hold of mangolds these days – not many farmers seem to grow them around here, but I know a good old-fashioned farmer who still grows a fair crop and I can rely on him to let me have a few for wine-making, providing that I present him with a bottle of the golden nectar when it's fit. I have to wait for the farmer to open his 'mango' bury in February or March before I can make this wine. When he does this, it is a joy to see the mangolds – they sit there warm and cosy in the earth bury and are all golden and yellow.

You need

> 5 lb mangolds
> 2 oranges
> 2 lemons
> 3 lb sugar
> 1 gallon water
> $\frac{1}{2}$ oz yeast

Wash the mangolds well but don't peel them. Cut them into small pieces, cover them with the water, bring to the boil, and simmer until tender. Strain the liquid and tip it back into the saucepan. Add the sugar and the rinds of the fruit and boil all this for about half an hour. Leave to cool. Add the juices from the fruit and sprinkle on the yeast. Cover and leave for 3 days. Strain, and then transfer the wine into the demijohn, fix the airlock and leave the wine to work, which will take about a month. Bottle off.

A lovely golden-coloured wine, a bit on the dry side, it can be drunk when it is 6 months old – but the longer you keep it the better it gets.

Mangold Wine Chicken Casserole

4 breasts of chicken, boned and skinned
1 pint mangold wine
Large bunch of mixed herbs including parsley, savory and
*   marjoram if possible, chopped fine*
3 large carrots, cut into matchstick shapes
2 medium onions, sliced thin
8 oz fresh mushrooms, sliced thin
1 green pepper, sliced thin
2 medium parsnips or 1 small celeriac (if available), sliced
*   thin to match carrots*
1 clove garlic, crushed or chopped very fine
Flour to dush chicken portions
2 tablespoons sunflower oil to fry chicken
Freshly ground black peppercorns and salt to season

Place chicken breasts into a glass or china dish and cover with the wine the night before you wish to cook the dish. Add to the chicken and wine the herbs and a little seasoning and put in a cool place overnight.

Next day, remove the chicken portions and dry with kitchen paper, reserving the juices of the marinade for later. Dust chicken breasts with flour and season well. Fry off chicken breasts in heated oil until crisp and golden on all sides. Remove the chicken from the heat and in the oil and juices that remain cook off the onions, mushrooms, parsnips (or celeriac), pepper and garlic, and fry gently until soft not brown. Mix in a teaspoon of flour to the vegetables and stir well, then add the marinade, stirring well to avoid the flour sticking to the pan. This should give you a reasonably thick sauce. Adjust seasoning, and pour mix into a casserole dish, add chicken and cook in medium oven for at least an hour – the longer you cook this dish the better the flavour.

Serve with Basmati rice and a green salad.

MARIGOLD

Marigold Wine

August is a good month in which to make this wine. Marigolds
take over my flower garden about this time, and from then until
early October the garden is ablaze with them, smothering everything else in sight. The good thing is that I can gather a gallon of
flower heads, and you can't see where I've picked them from! Try
to pick your marigolds on a sunny day, preferably at midday.
Then – it is said – you will be actually bottling sunshine, and the
bouquet of your wine will be much better for it.

> 1 gallon marigold flowers (measured in a quart jug)
> 1 gallon water
> 3 lb sugar
> ½ oz yeast
> 1 lemon
> 8 oz honey
> ½ pint white wine

Simmer the sugar, water and honey for about ten minutes, cool,
and add the marigold flowers, cutting off as much of the green frill
as possible. Add the juice, and the rind of the lemon. Sprinkle the
yeast on the top, cover and leave for 5 days. Strain and pour into
the demijohn, and continue as on page 4. When the time comes
to bottle this wine off, half a pint of any home-made wine added
to it will improve it no end.

The wine will be ready to drink in 8 months.

Marigold Vegetarian Pasties in Marigold Wine

8 marigold heads, picked early in the morning when they
    have first opened and the dew is still on them
4 oz Basmati rice
2 medium carrots, sliced like matchsticks
1 yellow pepper, sliced like matchsticks
1 medium onion, chopped very fine
8 pods of green peas, or a handful of frozen peas
A little green cabbage, chard or green vegetables, chopped
    into strips
¼ cucumber, sliced like matchsticks
A handful of mixed herbs including parsley, marjoram,
    thyme and summer savory, all chopped fine
2 tablespoons marigold wine
1 tablespoon sunflower oil
Enough shortcrust pastry to make up 4 pastry rounds the
    size of saucers for the pasties (usually 4 oz flour and 2 oz
    margarine are enough)
1 egg beaten well to wash over pastry before cooking
Freshly ground black peppercorns and salt to season

Heat the oil in large frying pan, add rice and gently cook for a
moment. Put in the vegetables and herbs and stir in well. Allow to
cook with the lid on the pan for a few moments. Add the marigold
wine, season and stir well; allow to cook for a few moments and
then add 4 dessertspoons water. Place lid on pan, turn the heat
right down and allow to simmer and cook gently.

Check the dish after about 8 minutes and if necessary add a little
more water. (You are aiming for a mix which consists of cooked
vegetables and separate yet soft cooked grains of rice. Be cautious
of adding too much liquid, or the end result could be sloppy and
quite unsuited to the dish you are preparing.) When the mix is
cooked and no liquid remains, adjust seasoning and set aside to
cool while you prepare the shortcrust pastry. Roll out the pastry,
cut 4 rounds using a saucer as a guide. Wash the outer rims of the

rounds with egg to ensure that a good seal will form when the sides are joined after the filling is added.

When the filling is reasonably cool add marigold petals and stir well in before spooning the mixture into the centre of the pastry shapes. Bring the opposite sides of the pastry rounds together and shape into pasties, wash with beaten egg, decorate if you wish and bake in a moderate oven until golden brown. This should take about 10 minutes. Serve as snack or main dish or take on a picnic.

Marigold Chicken with Marigold Wine

1 whole chicken or 4 chicken breasts
1 cup marigold petals free from green and stalks and taken
   from fresh marigolds picked that day
2 cloves garlic, crushed or chopped fine
1 pint marigold wine
4 oz fresh mushrooms, sliced fine
2 medium onions, sliced fine
4 large carrots sliced like matchsticks so that they resemble
   the marigold petals in shape
¼ cucumber, sliced into matchstick shapes
1 bunch fresh parsley, chopped fine
3 sprigs thyme, chopped fine
2 sprigs marjoram, chopped fine
Flour to dust chicken
3 tablespoons sunflower oil to fry chicken
Freshly ground black peppercorns and salt to season

If using a whole chicken, joint and skin and dust with seasoned flour. In a shallow pan, using the sunflower oil at a reasonably high heat, fry the chicken portions on all sides until they are golden brown but not completely cooked. Place half the marigold petals at the bottom of a large casserole dish and place the browned chicken portions on top.

In the remaining oil and juices of the meat fry off the garlic, mushrooms and onion until they are almost brown. Add the herbs and stir them in, then add one tablespoon of flour to this mix, stir it in, and allow to cook until soft brown. Pour in the wine and stir until you have obtained a smooth sauce. Season and pour the mixture onto the chicken portions.

Scatter the remaining petals on top of the mixture and cook with the lid on in a moderate oven for at least an hour, or until delicious smells from the oven tell you that the flavours are beginning to declare themselves. Serve with a green salad which has been decorated with marigold petals for effect.

MAY BLOSSOM

May Blossom Wine

When I make my May blossom wine, I always think of years ago. For haymaking time and May blossom blooming happened around the same time, when the farm workers went off with their scythes and sickles to mow the grass, always taking with them a stone jar of wine. The stone jar (and I have one) only had one handle on. The reason for this was that when a man had a drink from the jar, he tossed it up on to his left shoulder and moved his head to the left, enabling him to drink straight out of the jar. Jokes were often played on greedy drinkers. The working men would sometimes put new-born mice in with the wine. After swallowing the jar's contents, the drinker would comment, 'That wine's a bit thick, I reckon the farmer put too many hops in there.'

May blossom, or hawthorn blossom, grows freely during the months of May and June.

> 1 quart May blossom (free of all stalks and any green)
> 1 orange
> 3 lb 8 oz sugar
> 1 gallon water
> ½ oz yeast

Pick the blossoms when they are full out but not falling. Boil up the water, sugar and grated orange peel for about 15 minutes. Leave to cool a little and then add the May blossoms and the juice of the orange. When quite cool add the yeast. Cover the wine and leave for 4 days, stirring twice daily. Strain and continue as directed on page 4.

This makes a delicate pale creamy wine that is drinkable in 6 months.

Almond Nut Tart Flavoured with May Blossom Wine

For the pastry
4 oz butter or margarine
6 oz wholemeal flour
1 level tablespoon sunflower seeds
1 level tablespoon sesame seeds
A little cold water to mix

For the filling
4 oz ground almonds
4 oz flaked almonds
2 egg yolks, beaten well
1 tablespoon May blossom wine
Strawberry or raspberry jam to spread on pastry case
Caster sugar to sprinkle over top of tart

Prepare pastry by placing all dry ingredients into large bowl and rubbing well together until the mix resembles breadcrumbs. Add sufficient cold water to mix to a firm paste. Roll pastry out on a floured surface until it is thin enough to line an 8-inch pie dish. Line pie dish, cut away surplus pastry and keep for another occasion (will keep well in fridge for at least a couple of days). Spread the jam evenly and generously over pastry until completely covered. Mix ground almonds with egg yolks and wine and beat well until you have a smooth thick texture. Spoon this onto the jam and spread evenly. Sprinkle with flaked almonds and a little caster sugar. Bake in a moderate oven for about 20 minutes or until golden brown.

I remember one of my Witney aunts making a tart similar to this when I was a child, though she didn't put May blossom wine into the mix. She used to slice it up the moment it came out of the oven, and my brother and I would stand there in her kitchen clutching red-hot slices of tart which we puffed on so that they would be cool enough to eat quickly.

MEADOWSWEET

Meadowsweet Wine

Meadowsweet blooms freely all summer long, so you can pick your time to make it.

'Meadowsweet makes the heart merry', someone once wrote, and indeed this wine certainly does that. The foamy cream flowers have a sweet drowsy smell, which seems to embody the essence of the countryside in summer. You will need

> 1 gallon meadowsweet flowers
> 3 lb sugar
> 8 oz raisins
> 2 lemons
> 2 tablespoons cold strong tea
> 1 gallon water
> $\frac{1}{2}$ oz yeast

You need to pick these flowers before they are overblown. Be sure that no green is left on the florets. Place them in your wine-making bucket along with the sugar, raisins (split) and grated lemon rind. Pour over the boiling water, and stir well until the sugar has dissolved. Leave to get a little cool and then add the lemon juice and the cold tea. When really cool sprinkle on the yeast. Cover well and leave for 10 days. Strain and pour into your demijohn, proceed as on page 4.

A creamy-amber wine, this will be drinkable in 6 months.

Broad Bean Pâté with Meadowsweet Wine

I have chosen meadowsweet wine for this dish because it is a thin dry wine, but tea wine (see p.153) will do just as well. You will need

8 oz soft cream cheese
1 lb shelled broad beans
2 tablespoons meadowsweet wine
Freshly ground black peppercorns and salt to season

Place the beans in a pan of cold salted water, bring to the boil and simmer until almost cooked. Remove a spoonful of beans from the pot and refresh them in cool water while the rest continue to cook. When cooked (this won't take very long if the beans were picked fresh and young), strain and refresh with cool water. Soften the cheese with a fork. Place the cooked beans into a blender when cool, add meadowsweet wine and blend until pulp. Mix bean pulp and cheese together, then season and mix again.

Serve either as a thick dip decorated with beans which you removed earlier in the cooking process, or pipe into savoury pastry cases. Serve before the main meal, or use to accompany main meal.

I often use this dish for parties, especially as it contains no meat and satisfies the vegetarians. It is attractive, particularly when finished with the whole beans and perhaps a sprig of mint. But beware – I once served it at a garden party and found that the mix lost its initial colour, turning into a dull grey mix when exposed to the sun.

Salmon Steaks with Tarragon and Meadowsweet Wine

4 salmon steaks
$\frac{1}{2}$ pint meadowsweet wine
1 bunch spring onions, chopped very fine
1 bunch fresh tarragon, half of which can be chopped fine,
*   the rest saved for the garnish*
4 sprigs parsley, chopped fine
Freshly ground peppercorns and salt to season
Juice of half a lemon (optional)

In a large frying pan place the salmon steaks, the meadowsweet wine, the onions, parsley and chopped tarragon, and season lightly. Place a lid over the pan and allow to cook gently over a moderate heat until the fish is cooked. This usually takes at least 15 to 20 minutes, but if the steaks have been cut thin remember they will cook much more quickly. Remove the fish carefully from the pan and keep warm.

Bring the juices left in the pan to boiling point and allow to simmer for a while without the lid until they have reduced in volume by at least a third. Adjust seasoning, and add a squeeze of lemon to the sauce if you want to bring out an extra tang. Place salmon steaks on serving dish, pour over the wine mix and serve with a garnish of fresh tarragon.

Fresh Apricots Poached with Meadowsweet Flowers and Wine

1 lb fresh apricots, cut in half and stoned
6 meadowsweet flower heads picked when they are in full
* flower*
½ pint meadowsweet wine
Sugar to taste

Place the wine, apricots and flower heads together in a saucepan and simmer the mixture gently for long enough to cook the fruit right through, but not so much that it will fall to bits when touched. Taste and if necessary add a little sugar. Meadowsweet wine tends to be rather thin, and often quite dry, which is great if the apricots are ripe, sweet and juicy, but not so good if they are a little on the firm side and rather sour.

Remove the meadowsweet heads and allow the dessert to cool in a refrigerator. Serve chilled with sweet biscuits.

MIXED FRUIT

Mixed Fruit Wine

This wine can be made in June or July. When the soft fruit have passed their best and I think I've made enough jam and jelly, then I use the 'tail end' fruit to make a super mixed fruit wine, which includes gooseberries, raspberries, black- and redcurrants, and, if there are any left, a few strawberries.

> *4 lb mixed fruit (they don't have to be in equal quantities)*
> *1 gallon boiling water*
> *4 lb sugar*
> *2 lemons*
> *½ oz yeast*

Top and tail the fruit and place in your wine-making container. Add the boiling water, cover and leave for 3 days, stirring 3 times a day. Strain, put back into your container, and add the sugar, the juice and the grated rinds of the lemons. Stir well until the sugar has dissolved, and then sprinkle on the yeast. Cover again, and leave for a week. Strain and tip the wine into the demijohn, and continue as on page 4.

This makes a delicious fruity wine, sweet and a lovely colour, a great favourite with everyone. It should be ready to drink in 6 months.

Apples Baked in Mixed Fruit Wine

4 lovely firm Bramley apples
½ pint mixed fruit wine
4 oz sultanas
4 oz brown sugar

Prepare each apple by coring and cutting the skin around the centre of the apple to allow it to expand and puff out to its full glory while cooking. Place the apples in a baking dish and fill the core of each apple with sultanas and sugar, packing the mix in tight. Pour the wine over the apples and allow it to cascade onto the tray. Throw any sultanas and sugar that are over onto the tray so that the wine can soak in.

Bake in a moderate oven for 20 to 30 minutes. The baking time will depend upon the texture and the size of the apples, but you will know when they are done by their wonderful smell and the sight of the powdery white flesh puffing itself up and out through the cut. Serve with thick Jersey cream or yoghurt, spooning the sauce in the bottom of the tray onto each apple.

A Tale of Woe

My Auntie Sarah was a great wine-maker. She was also a good
chapel-going body, too. One hot summer I remember she had a couple
of lay preachers staying with her for a few days. They were going
round to some of the remote villages to preach the gospel and made my
auntie's home their temporary headquarters. Both were very much the
'holier than thou' type and firmly believed that any form of 'drink' was
a sure passport to hell.

Before they arrived at the farm we carefully moved all the bottles
and casks of wine up into a loft over the kitchen. The farm had once
been a mill and this loft was where the flour had been stored. We had
to handle it very gently because some of the wine was still at the
fermenting stage, but at least it was out of sight.

All we heard from the lay preachers was that hell fire and
damnation would surely be the fate of anyone who took any sort of
intoxicating drink. My uncle would catch my eye and look
heavenwards as if to say, 'How much longer have we got to put up
with this?'

But suddenly their visit was cut short. The afternoon was very hot,
distant thunder rolled round the hills. There was not a breath of air
anywhere, and the worthy gentlemen were leading off for the
umpteenth time about the sins of the world, and how they were going
to convert everybody, when the air was shattered with a loud report,
then another and another. Up jumped the black-coated lay preachers,
eyes blazing, arms flung heavenwards.

'There are the warning notes,' called one.

'Yes, hell fire and damnation!' shouted the other,
'Judgement on all sinners!'

Just at that moment a red, gory substance started pouring down the walls
and onto the white, scrubbed stone floor and settled in a puddle at one of the
visitors' feet, and a strong fruity, winey smell filled the room. I took one look
at my red-faced aunt and we both went off to get buckets and house flannels to
sop up the mess. The visitors stamped out of the house and up the road
toward the next village, and we never saw them again.

The only damnation came from my uncle because his favourite wine
(raspberry, red- and blackcurrant) had ended up all over the kitchen floor.

101

MULBERRY

Mulberry Wine

4 lb mulberries
3 lb 8 oz sugar
1 gallon water
1 oz yeast

Place the mulberries in your wine-making bucket and pour the gallon of boiling water over them. Cover and leave for 4 or 5 days, stirring daily. Strain onto the sugar and stir well until all is dissolved. Add the yeast and cover well. Leave for about a week. Strain off again into your demijohn, fix airlock and proceed as on page 4.

This is a lovely full-bodied wine and super with meat dishes.

Mulberry Wine Pudding

2 lb mulberries
3 dessertspoons runny honey
1 medium-sized loaf which is at least a day old, preferably
  granary or wholemeal
½ pint mulberry wine
2 teaspoons arrowroot
A little butter to grease pudding dish

Place mulberries, honey and wine into a saucepan and gently simmer over a low heat until the mulberries have cooked. Strain mulberries and retain the juice for the sauce. Remove all the crusts from the bread and slice into reasonably thick slices, then halve diagonally.

Grease a pudding dish and line with the wedges of bread, slightly overlapping one on top of the other so that there are no cracks. Pour in the cooked mulberries, and press down firmly with a wooden spoon. Using more slices of bread, cover the mulberries completely and place a plate on top. Weigh the plate down with a heavy weight (large tin or 2 lb weight if possible) and allow to stand in a refrigerator for at least half a day.

Make the sauce by bringing the juices to the boil and thickening with a little arrowroot that has been thinned with wine. Stir well until the mix reaches a suitable texture and serve chilled alongside a jug of thick Jersey cream or yoghurt. Turn the pudding out onto a flat plate – it should keep its shape perfectly if you have allowed it to stand long enough.

NETTLE

Nettle Wine

So many things are free and easily gathered in the countryside, and there are always plenty of stinging nettles around – so why not make the most of them. This wine is best made any time from April until the end of May, because that's when the nettles are young and green. It is not to be confused with 'nettle beer' which is quite a different thing and can be found in the 'summer drinks' section.

1 quart nettle tops
2 lemons
4 lb sugar
½ oz root ginger
1 gallon water
½ oz yeast

Rinse the nettle tops under the tap, place them in a large saucepan, and cover with water. Add the rind of the lemons and the bruised ginger. Bring to the boil and simmer for 30 minutes; if you think that you have lost much liquid in boiling, make up to the gallon with cold water. Put the sugar into your wine-making bucket, pour over the hot liquid and add the juices of the lemons. Stir and leave to cool before adding the yeast. Cover and leave for 3 days before straining the wine off into your demijohn. Continue as directed on page 4.

This will be a pale greeny amber wine, drinkable in 6 months. Apart from being very pleasant to drink, it is also good for clearing the blood and easing the digestion.

Nettle Soup

1 cup nettle wine

A generous supply of meaty beef bones to which you can add chicken and game bones for extra flavour

A bunch of freshly picked herbs, including if possible parsley, thyme, marjoram, winter or summer savory and borage leaves

8 oz fresh mushrooms, sliced thin

3 medium onions, sliced thin

4 sticks of celery, chopped fine

A small bunch of nettles, carefully washed and finely chopped (wear rubber gloves to avoid the stings and use only the tender young leaves which you should remove from the stalks)

2 oz Basmati rice

Freshly ground black peppercorns and salt to season

Bake the bones in a very hot oven until they are crisp and brown – this will give you the flavour and colour that you need for a good rich stock. Place the bones in a saucepan and cover with twice as much water as you will need in the end. Add to this the herbs, 4 oz of the mushrooms, 2 of the onions, and half the celery. Season well, but not too well (remember this liquid will reduce as it cooks). Allow to come to the boil, take off any scum that may form on the surface and simmer gently for at least 3 hours – the longer the better as far as flavour is concerned (I often let this simmer all day and way into the night).

When the liquid has reduced itself by half and you are happy with the flavour, strain it into another large saucepan. Add the nettles, the remaining mushrooms and onions, add the celery and the rice to the stock and allow to simmer again until the added ingredients have cooked through. Add the nettle wine at the last moment, adjust seasoning and serve with fresh crusty brown bread.

I have often added chunks of boiled rabbit to this dish in order to create a really meaty soup and I've found that the flavours blend very well.

OAK LEAF

Oak Leaf Wine

The leaves of the oak tree should be picked when they are young and at their best – about the third week in June is quite a good time.

> 1 gallon oak leaves (measured in a jug)
> 3 lb 8 oz sugar
> 2 sweet oranges
> 2 lemons
> 1 gallon water
> ½ oz yeast

Wipe the oak leaves with a cloth, then put them into your wine-making container. Boil up the sugar with the water and pour it over them. Cover and leave overnight. Then add the juices from the oranges and lemons, and the yeast. Cover again for 2 days, then strain and tip the wine into your demijohn. Carry on as directed on page 4.

A medium-dry white wine with a good bouquet, drinkable after 6 months.

Quail Braised in Oak Leaf Wine

4 quail, plucked and oven ready
8 oz fresh mushrooms, sliced quite thin
6 juniper berries, crushed
8 oz fresh ham carved off the bone, cut into matchstick
  shapes
2 dessertspoons sunflower oil to fry quail
Enough flour to dust quail before frying
Handful fresh parsley, chopped fine
½ pint oak leaf wine
Freshly ground black peppercorns and salt to season

Wash the quail, dry with kitchen paper and dust all over with flour. Put the quail in a shallow pan and fry in oil, turning gently until each side is golden brown. Remove the quail from the pan, place them in a casserole dish and keep warm. To the remaining oil and juices add the crushed juniper berries, mushrooms, parsley and a little seasoning and fry gently until the mushrooms are cooked but not brown. Add slices of ham to this mix and pour on the wine, allow to sizzle and bubble for a moment and then pour entire mix over the quail. Adjust seasoning.

Place lid on casserole dish and cook in a medium oven for about 1½ hours or until the delicious smell of juniper berries and oak leaf wine tell you something very interesting is going on in your oven. Serve as is – traditionally quail are served whole.

Note that quails are one of the smallest of wild birds and so country people often serve at least two for each portion. But the number of birds you serve is up to you. If you cook a good selection of fresh green vegetables alongside the quail I believe one bird is more than enough.

ORANGE

Orange Wine

This is quite an expensive wine which acts as a tonic and is recommended to people suffering from anaemia – people who work in the orange groves and eat plenty of the fruit, seldom suffer from influenza or anaemia.

12 oranges
1 gallon water
2 lb sugar
$\frac{1}{2}$ oz yeast

Cut the oranges into thin slices, remove the pips, and put them into your wine-making container. Pour the boiling water over them. Cover and leave for 5 days, stirring daily. Strain and add the sugar, stir well, and add just a sprinkling of yeast. Leave for a further 3 days, strain and tip all into your demijohn and continue as on page 4.

This wine will be drinkable in 3 months, but of course it will mature and improve if left longer.

Chestnut and Orange Soup

1 lb fresh chestnuts
1 tablespoon flour
2 oz unsalted butter
2 large carrots, chopped fine
2 medium onions, chopped fine
4 oz mushrooms, sliced fine
4 dessertspoons orange wine
Rind from 2 large oranges, grated fine for garnish
4 sprigs parsley, chopped fine
2 pints beefy rich stock (if you cheat and use a stock cube,
  remember that you must reduce the amount of salt in the
  seasoning)
Freshly ground black peppercorns and salt to season

Prepare the chestnuts by making a small cut in the outer skin of each one and boiling for 5 minutes before peeling. Melt the butter in a large saucepan but do not allow it to go brown. Add the carrots, onions, mushrooms and parsley and fry gently together until soft brown but not overdone. Stir the flour into the cooked vegetables to make a paste. Let this mix brown just a little, but not too much, and then stir in the stock, wine and chestnuts. Adjust seasoning and bring to the boil.

Allow the soup to simmer for at least 1½ hours or until the chestnuts are well and truly cooked and the basic flavours have fused together to form an appetizing taste. Allow to cool sufficiently to pass the mix through a sieve or put into a blender. Reduce the mix to a fine purée and return to the saucepan. Add the grated rind of 1 orange and allow the purée to heat through again; if it is too thick you can always add just a drop more orange wine. Use the rind of the remaining orange as a final garnish on the tureen or on each soup bowl.

Serve round the fire on a chilly day with lots of crusty brown bread.

Warm Pigeon Salad with Orange Wine Dressing

8 pigeon breasts
2 teaspoons sunflower oil to fry pigeon breasts
Enough mixed green salad for 4 including lettuce, cucumber,
*   sliced green peppers, chives, cherville and dill if possible.*
1 small onion, chopped very fine
Juice of 1 fresh orange
4 tablespoons orange wine
1 teaspoon mustard powder
4 oz pecan nuts or walnuts
2 oz raisins
1 cup sunflower oil
Freshly ground black peppercorns and salt to season

Soak the raisins in the orange wine overnight, strain and retain the liquid. Wash and prepare salad and keep to one side but do not refrigerate. Prepare sauce for salad by gently frying the onion in a small amount of oil, but do not brown. Mix dry mustard with a little of the wine to form a paste, add to the rest of the wine and pour into the pan. As the mix begins to bubble, add the juice of the orange and stir well and allow to reduce its volume by at least a third. Adjust seasoning.

Remove the pan from the heat, season and whisk in the oil, allow to stand while you cook the pigeon breasts by gently frying them in a little oil. It helps to flatten the breasts slightly before cooking to ensure even cooking throughout. Remove breasts when cooked and allow to stand while you add the sauce mix to the juices left in the pan; allow to cook for a few moments, then strain. Assemble by slicing breasts into strips and placing them attractively on top of the salad to which you have added the nuts and raisins.

Spoon sauce over the completed dish and serve immediately. Garnish with chervile.

On a warm summer's day this makes an ideal main course if served with slices of warm granary bread, but it can equally well double as a first course if you want to offer a more substantial meal.

PARSLEY

Parsley Wine

This wine can be made at almost any time of the year – whenever you have sufficient parsley growing in your garden.

> *1 lb parsley (free from stalks)*
> *2 oranges*
> *2 lemons*
> *4 lb sugar*
> *A piece of root ginger as big as a walnut*
> *1 gallon water*
> *$\frac{1}{2}$ oz yeast*

Put your parsley into your wine bucket and pour a gallon of boiling water over it. Cover and let it stand for 2 days. Strain and boil up the liquor for 20 minutes along with the ginger and the grated rinds of the fruit. Pour the hot liquor onto the sugar, add the juice and when cool add the yeast. Leave for 4 days. Strain, pour into the demijohn, and proceed as on page 4.

This wine should be ready in 6 months, but of course it will improve if you can manage to keep it longer, as all wines improve if kept for a year or more.

Parsley Brandy Wine

Parsley makes a delightful amber-coloured sweet wine, which would improve any meal; and the fact that the leaves contain vitamin C means that it is bound to 'do a body a power of good'. So here's a recipe which is very simple and gives a wonderful result.

> *8 oz parsley leaves (free from stalks)*
> *4 oz raisins (these give the wine a 'brandy' colour)*
> *2 oranges*
> *2 lemons*
> *3 lb 8 oz sugar*
> *1 oz root ginger (bruised)*
> *1 gallon water*
> *$\frac{1}{2}$ oz yeast*

Wash the parsley and tip it into a large saucepean. Cover with the water, bring to the boil and simmer for 30 minutes, keeping the water topped up to 1 gallon. Strain and tip into your wine-making container and add the bruised ginger, raisins (split), sugar, rinds and juice of the lemons and oranges. Stir until the sugar has dissolved. When cool add the yeast. Cover with a cloth and leave for a week. Then strain again into the demijohn and proceed as on page 4. Bottle off.

This wine will be drinkable in 4 months and is truly outstanding among home-made wines. It has a most delicate bouquet and makes a delicious dinner or lunch-time wine.

Don't be disheartened if your parsley seed is a long time coming through. It is said that it goes down three times to the devil before it decides to grow.

Pork and Parsley Wine Casserole

1 lb pork, chopped into 1-inch cubes with fat removed
$\frac{1}{4}$ pint parsley wine
1 large bunch parsley, chopped fine
$\frac{1}{4}$ pint rich brown stock (if you cheat and use a stock cube
  for this, remember to add less salt to the dish)
$\frac{1}{2}$ cucumber, chopped into matchstick shapes
4 carrots, chopped fine
4 oz mushrooms, use whole
1 green pepper, chopped into matchstick shapes
$\frac{1}{4}$ pint single cream
4 tablespoons flour
3 tablespoons sunflower oil to fry chops
$\frac{1}{2}$ teaspoon ground mace
Freshly ground black peppercorns and salt to season

Cut away all the fat from the pork and dice into cubes. Flour and season the pork cubes and place into heated oil. Fry pork cubes until crisp and golden brown. Add parsley, carrots, mushrooms and sliced pepper to pork cubes and stir well, reducing heat so they cook but do not brown. Add the flour and ground mace and stir in well until it begins to take on a light brown colour. Add the parsley wine and stock gradually, stirring as you do so to achieve a smooth sauce. Season, and our whole mix into a large casserole dish. Cook with lid on in moderate oven for at least 1$\frac{1}{2}$ hours. Adjust seasoning when cooked and stir in the cream at the last moment, but while the dish is still bubbling slightly.

At the very last moment add the cucumber slices for just long enough for them to warm through but not cook. If these are piled carelessly on top of the dish they make a very attractive finish. Their simple clean flavour works well with this sauce and adds just the right balance and contrast.

PARSNIP

Parsnip Wine

The first wine I make, at the beginning of the year, is parsnip. This is when they are at their best, when the frosts have turned some of the starch into sugar. However, one old lady I know only ever uses young parsnips.

For anyone who has lost their appetite, a glass of parsnip wine a day will soon lead to an improvement in their eating habits. Some people call parsnip wine 'mock sherry', for it looks and often tastes like it.

> *4 lb parsnips*
> *1 gallon water*
> *4 lb demerara sugar (3 lb for a dry wine)*
> *2 lemons*
> *2 grapefruit*
> *$\frac{1}{2}$ oz yeast*

Scrub the parsnips clean but do not peel. Cut up into chunks and place in a large saucepean along with the cold water and the thinly sliced but unpeeled lemons and grapefruit. Cook until the parsnips are tender but not mushy. Strain the liquor onto the sugar and stir well. When cool, sprinkle on the yeast. Cover with a thick cloth and leave for 10 days. Strain, tip into your demijohn and proceed as on page 4.

Try not to drink this until it has stood for a year. If you make it in January, it should be just fit to drink at Christmastime.

Pheasant with Parsnip Wine

A brace of pheasants
2 tablespoons sunflower oil to fry pheasants and vegetables
2 medium onions, chopped very fine
4 large parsnips, roughly chopped
half a celery, roughly chopped
2 leaves of lovage if available
Flour to dust pheasants before browning
¼ pint parsnip wine
¼ pint rich double cream
¼ pint rich brown stock made from game or pheasant
*   bones if possible*
Freshly ground black peppercorns and salt to season

Clean pheasants leaving whole if you wish, but you can portion them if preferred. Heat the oil in large frying pan and fry celery, onions and parsnips until almost brown. Remove fried vegetables and place at the bottom of a large casserole dish. In the remaining juices fry the pheasants; it may be necessary to add a little more oil to the pan at this stage. When the meat is brown on all sides remove and place on top of the cooked vegetables.

Add the parsnip wine and stock to the remaining juices in the pan and allow to bubble for a moment before seasoning. Add lovage leaves to the dish at this stage if you managed to obtain some. Pour this liquid over the meat and vegetables and cook in a medium oven for at least 1¼ hours – the slower the better.

Remove pheasants from the casserole mix and keep warm while you prepare the sauce. Allow sauce to cool slightly so that it can be blended together in a food processor to form a purée. (Celery can be stubborn and stringy at times, so perhaps you will have to strain this mix to achieve the perfect sauce.) Put the purée into a saucepan and allow to simmer for a few moments, adjust seasoning, and then whisk in the cream before removing from the heat. Either pour this mix back onto the pheasants and serve that way, or use as the basic sauce on the dinner plate on which you arrange the portions of meat.

This dish has a rich flavour and is filling, so serve simple green vegetables alongside it.

PEA POD

Pea Pod Wine

Summer is the time for making this one.

This is an easy wine to make, and it's a pity to throw those lovely fresh green pea pods onto the compost heap when they could be made into a delightful wine that is supposed to resemble hock.

> 5 lb pea pods
> 3 lb sugar
> Juice of a large grapefruit
> 1 gallon water
> $\frac{1}{2}$ oz yeast

Wash the pods and boil them up in the gallon of water until they are quite tender. Strain and add the sugar to the liquid. When nearly cold add the juice of the grapefruit, and then the yeast. Next day tip the wine into your demijohn and continue as on page 4.

Drinkable within 4 months.

Pea Pod Wine Vegetable Stir Fry

Half a bunch of new carrots, sliced fine
1 bunch spring onions, chopped small
1 lb fresh peas, shelled
6 baby sweetcorn if available (these are optional, but get
    them if you can – they add colour and contrast to the dish
    and taste terrific)
6 small new potatoes, cooked in boiling minted water and
    chopped into wedges
4 oz mange tout
8 oz broad beans, shelled
8 oz broad beans, chopped into inch bits skin and all (only
    attempt this if the skins are tender and the beans young)
1 large bunch of fresh parsley, chopped fine
2 sprigs marjoram, chopped fine
1 sprig mint, chopped fine
8 oz tomatoes, skinned and chopped (only skin if they are
    not freshly picked)
½ cucumber, sliced into matchstick shapes
1 clove garlic, chopped fine
4 oz pine nut kernels (or sliced almonds)
2 drops soy sauce
¼ pint pea pod wine
3 dessertspoons sunflower oil
Freshly ground black peppercorns and salt to season

Chop and slice all the vegetables according to their shape. Heat the oil in a large frying pan and add the carrots, sweetcorn, potatoes, broad beans, spring onions and garlic. Allow these to cook through for a few moments, stirring all the time. Add all the other vegetables and herbs, putting the tomatoes in last, as their water content will take away the frying power of the oil. Add two drops soy sauce and season, remembering to go easy on the salt as the soy is salty. Add the wine and stir well, throw in the nuts, turn off the heat and place a lid on top of the pan for a few moments.

You are aiming for vegetables which are still crisp yet have taken up the flavour of the wine, the soy sauce and the herbs. You will notice that the mint adds a delightful edge to this dish. The nutty aftertaste of the wine will make its own statement.

Rice is the most suitable extra to serve with this dish, though it can be served with hot crusty bread too.

*The juicy fruit of blackcurrants makes a health-giving wine and
produces delicious desserts (page 34)*

Harvest home – rabbit pie with potato wine (page 124)

A super stir fry – using pea pod wine (page 117)

Cherry ripe – cherry wine – cherry cream (page 46)

*Something for the vegetarian – pasties and wine make a nice
tasty snack (page 145)*

*Harvest fruits of elderberries and apples combine to make this
spiced elderberry and apple tart (page 66)*

*Sun-kissed strawberries and strawberry wine make this
delicious trifle (page 152)*

*Celebrating the last of the summer wine in Mollie's garden –
surrounded by the ingredients for this year's brew*

PEAR

Pear Wine or Perry

You can make this wine during August and September. Whether you call this pear wine or perry, the end product is much the same. Although pears are not credited with any great medicinal value, it is said that sufferers from gout or those with gout tendencies should drink pear wine. The recipe is simple.

> *4 lb ripe pears*
> *3 lb sugar*
> *1 gallon water*
> *$\frac{1}{4}$ oz yeast*

Remove the stalks from the fruit. Put the pears into your wine-making vessel and pour cold water over them. Cover and leave for a week, stirring a couple of times a day, pressing the fruit against the side of your bucket with a wooden spoon. Strain off, add the sugar to the juice sprinkle on the yeast and leave in your bucket for a further 4 days, with the wine *well* covered. Tip all into your demijohn, and proceed as directed on page 4.

Last year I made 2 separate gallons of pear wine, the second gallon 2 days after the first. I used exactly the same method, but the first gallon cleared within 2 weeks of being in the demijohn, while the second batch remained quite cloudy. I mentioned this to an 89-year-old wine-making neighbour, and he suggested adding to my cloudy gallon a spoonful of *his* 'pectolytic enzyme', which he had bought from the chemist – which I did. Whether that did the job or, given time, the wine had cleared itself, I shall never know, but it turned out lovely and clear and is a very nice wine.

Perry should be drinkable in 5 months, but will improve if it is kept a year or more.

Poached Pears

*1 fresh pear for each person and perhaps a few extra for
  seconds*
½ pint pear wine
1 drop edible food dye (optional)

Peel the pears, cut in half and core carefully. Place pears in a
shallow pan with sufficient wine to cover. Gently bring to the
boil, then allow the pears to simmer. Cover with a lid to stop
evaporation – this is one dish where we are not going to reduce the
liquid.

When cooked remove from heat and cool. If you wish the pears
can be served hot, but I find them nicer if they are chilled and
served with yoghurt or rich thick Jersey cream. Extra colour can
be added to the pears by putting a little food dye onto them at the
very last moment before serving. But remember if you do this to
keep the pears and their juice apart or all will be lost and the colour
will weep into the liquid.

This dish is so simple you may feel guilty that it has taken so
little effort to produce. But don't worry – remember that some of
the best flavours come from simple ingredients that have not lost
their original taste by being mixed with others.

PLUM

Plum Wine

August and early September are the best times for making plum wine. Plums halved and stoned freeze well, so if you haven't time to make the wine while the plums are fresh, freeze some and make it later in the year.

> 3 lb stoned plums
> 3 lb sugar
> 1 gallon water
> ½ oz yeast

Put the plums into your bucket and pour a gallon of boiling water over them. Cover and leave for 5 days, stirring a couple of times daily. Strain, and pour the liquid back into the bucket. Stir in the sugar and keep stirring until the sugar has dissolved, then sprinkle on the yeast and cover the wine with a thick cloth. Stand the wine in a warm place – in the kitchen window might do. Strain again and tip all the wine into your demijohn. Proceed as on page 4.

Plums make a lovely rich, red, fruity wine, drinkable after 6 months. If you prefer your wine not so sweet, only use 2 lb 4 oz of sugar.

Venison Liver with Red Plum Wine Sauce

◇◇◇

1 lb thinly sliced venison liver
½ pint red plum wine
8 red plums, poached and set aside for garnish
2 dessertspoons sunflower oil to cook liver and a little for the
sauce
1 tablespoon caster sugar
2 dessertspoons of any home-made wine which has acquired
a sherry-like flavour – tea wine is ideal
1 teaspoon arrowroot or cornflour to thicken sauce
1 bunch spring onions, chopped neatly and fine
Parsley or watercress to garnish
A little flour to dust liver before frying
Freshly ground black peppercorns and salt to season

First make your sauce by frying off the spring onions in oil over a gentle heat so that they become soft but not brown. Add sugar and stir for a moment but do not brown. Add sherry-like wine and red plum wine and allow to bubble for a moment before lowering the heat and adjusting the seasoning. Mix arrowroot or cornflour with a little plum wine and pour this into the mix, stirring all the time as the liquid thickens. Set the sauce aside while you fry off the liver slices.

First season the liver and dust with a small amount of flour before adding to heated oil and cooking gently until the slices are golden brown on both sides but not overcooked so they become tough. Pour a little sauce onto each plate and arrange the liver slices on top of the sauce, but do not cover them with the sauce. Garnish with poached plums and a touch of parsley or watercress.

This sauce is quite rich and stands alone. You really must select the vegetables to go with this dish with care so that they do not overpower the sauce, for there is nothing worse than several strong flavours fighting with each other for attention.

POTATO

Potato Wine

There are several ways of making potato wine, all of which involve mixing in other ingredients such as prunes, raisins, figs and wheat. I think potato and raisin is my favourite – the end product could easily be taken for a hock.

> *6 old raw potatoes the size of eggs*
> *2 oranges*
> *3 lemons*
> *4 lb sugar*
> *8 oz raisins*
> *1 gallon water*
> *½ oz dried yeast or a piece of yeast as big as a walnut*

Thinly slice the oranges and lemons and remove the pips, cut up the potatoes into chunks, and pull open the raisins. Put into your bucket with the sugar and pour over the gallon of boiling water. Stir well when cool. Sprinkle the yeast on top, cover and leave for 10 days. Strain and tip into your demijohn and proceed as on page 4.

This whisky-coloured wine is best left a year before drinking.

Rabbit Pie with Potato Wine

*Enough shortcrust pastry to make pie crust (amount will
    depend on width of your dish, but I usually find that 4 oz
    flour and 2 oz margarine provide enough)*
1 egg to wash over pastry before cooking, beaten well
1 rabbit, quartered
½ pint potato wine
*Generous bunch of mixed herbs including tarragon and
    parsley if possible, chopped fine*
2 large onions, chopped fine
4 large carrots, chopped fine
4 sticks celery, chopped fine
*4 medium-sized potatoes, diced small but not so small as to
    vanish in the pot*
Freshly ground black peppercorns and salt to season

Place rabbit quarters in a large saucepan, cover with wine, and add
sufficient salted water to cover. Cook gently after bringing mix to
the boil, allowing to simmer for at least 1 hour – until the meat
starts to fall off the bone. When cooked remove the meat from the
pot, and strain the liquid into another pan to which you add the
remaining ingredients. Adjust seasoning.

While the vegetables are cooking, remove the meat from the
bone. (Be careful, take your time, for there are some very small
and dangerous little bones in rabbit which should *not* be added to
the final dish!) Place cooked rabbit into pie dish, spoon on
vegetables and sufficient stock to cover, but not too much – the
pastry shouldn't go soggy as it cooks. Cover with pastry, decorate
with pastry leaves for extra finish, wash with egg and bake in a
moderate oven until the pastry is golden brown.

Rabbit used to be considered a poor man's dish and people
avoided using it for special parties a few years ago. But today it
can stand proudly alongside any of the classic dishes and is as tasty
as chicken and certainly more tender than some wild game meats.

The only thing to watch is the size of your rabbit. Sometimes it
is necessary to buy two for this dish if they are slender.

Fish Broth with Potato Wine

1 lb 8 oz fresh white fish (I find whiting best for this dish,
    but any firm-fleshed white fish will do, so long as it
    provides you with bones and skin to make a good strong
    stock)
3 large tomatoes, skinned and chopped fine
1 medium onion, chopped fine
4 oz celeriac, chopped into $\frac{1}{2}$-inch cubes
4 large potatoes, chopped into $\frac{1}{2}$-inch cubes
4 oz fresh mushrooms, sliced thin
2 cloves garlic, crushed or chopped very fine
4 strands saffron if you can afford it and really want to lift
    the dish
Handful fresh herbs including parsley, thyme and chives,
    chopped fine
2 tablespoons olive oil (do try to get olive oil if possible, as
    it really does make a difference to this dish)
$\frac{1}{2}$ pint potato wine
Freshly ground black peppercorns and salt to season

Fillet and skin the fish. Place all the trimmings, including head and
bones, into a saucepean with a pint of cold water. Simmer gently
for about 20 minutes, skimming off any scum from the top as it
cooks. Strain the fish stock and set aside in a cool place.

In another pan, heat the olive oil and add the onions, potatoes,
celeriac and mushrooms and cook gently until they are all soft but
not brown. To this add tomatoes, garlic and chopped herbs,
stirring well as you do so. Add stock and potato wine and bring
the lot to the boil. Adjust seasoning and lower the heat, allowing
the broth to simmer for at least 30 minutes.

Cut the fish into small cubes and add to the pot with the saffron.
Bring to the boil, then lower the heat again and allow the dish to
continue cooking gently for a few moments to allow the fish to
cook. Taste again and adjust seasoning if necessary. Serve as soon
as the fish is cooked.

QUINCE

Quince Wine

Autumn is the time to make this wine.

This is a simple wine to make, and a very pleasant one. Sufferers from rheumatism and gout can drink it freely knowing that it will not irritate their complaint.

> *2 dozen quince*
> *1 gallon water*
> *2 lemons*
> *3 lb sugar*
> *½ oz yeast*

Peel the quince and chop them up quite small. Cover with water, bring to the boil and simmer for about 20 minutes. When cool, strain and tip the liquor into your bucket, adding the sugar, the juice of the lemons and the yeast. Cover and leave for 3 or 4 days. Tip all into your demijohn and continue as on page 4.

Quince is a slow-maturing wine and is better if left for at least a year before drinking.

Rabbit Poached in Quince Wine with Redcurrant and Quince Garnish

2 rabbits skinned, portioned and boned as far as possible
1 pint quince wine
2 large quince, peeled
8 oz frozen redcurrants (fresh redcurrants are not available
when quince are harvested, but they freeze well)
2 medium onions, chopped fine
2 teaspoons redcurrant jelly
2 sprigs thyme, chopped fine
Small bunch parsley, chopped fine
Flour to dust rabbit before cooking
2 tablespoons sunflower oil to fry rabbit portions
Freshly ground black peppercorns and salt to season

Prepare rabbit portions, removing as many bones as possible. Dust rabbit portions with seasoned flour and fry gently in the sunflower oil until golden brown, using a cooking pot and not a frying pan. Lower the heat and add onions and quince slices and continue to cook gently until the onions and quince are soft but not brown. Add wine and herbs and allow to bubble for a moment, season and lower the heat, allowing the whole dish to cook on the stove with a lid on the saucepan for between 1 and $1\frac{1}{2}$ hours. The flesh of the rabbit should fall away from the bone easily when it is cooked.

Remove the rabbit for a moment and keep it warm while you finish the sauce. Reduce the liquid in volume by bringing it to a rapid boil without the lid on. It should be reduced by at least a third. Adjust seasoning, add redcurrant jelly and stir well. Add redcurrants at the very last moment, just before returning the rabbit portions to the pot to heat through again.

Serve with a garnish of redcurrants if you have some frozen on the stalk, and a little greenery, for instance, parsley, watercress or perhaps lemon balm.

RASPBERRY

Raspberry Wine

June and July are the best months to make this wine from fresh fruit. But raspberries freeze well, and wine made from frozen fruit turns out as good as that made from fresh raspberries.

> *3 lb raspberries*
> *3 lb sugar*
> *1 gallon water*
> *½ oz yeast*

Choose firm ripe raspberries. Place them in a bucket and pour over them a gallon of boiling water. Cover with a cloth and leave for 4 days, stirring daily. Strain and tip the wine back into your wine-making bucket, add the sugar and stir well. Sprinkle on the yeast and cover again and stand the wine in a warm place. Leave for a week and then strain again and pour the wine into your demijohn. Proceed as on page 4.

Raspberries make one of the most aromatic fruit wines. It is also very refreshing, a rosé-type wine that is delicious served with your sweet on a summer evening after you have kept it for a year; but it is drinkable after 6 months.

Pot Roast Pheasant in Raspberry Wine

A brace of pheasants well hung, and prepared but left whole
½ pint raspberry wine
8 oz fresh mushrooms, chopped very fine
4 sticks celery, chopped very fine
Enough frozen raspberries to stuff inside each bird (unfortunately raspberries are not in season at the same time as pheasants, so one or the other has to be frozen and as the raspberries freeze so well, let it be raspberries)
2 medium onions, chopped very fine
Generous bunch of mixed herbs, including thyme and parsley, chopped fine
4 oz breadcrumbs to mix with raspberries
4 lovage leaves (if available) to give extra lift to the flavour of finished dish, chopped fine
Freshly ground black peppercorns and salt to season

Place prepared pheasants in large glass or china bowl to which you have added the herbs and wine; leave overnight in a cool place to marinade, making sure that the meat is covered with wine completely (add more wine if needed at this stage). Remove pheasants from marinade and stuff with (thawed) raspberries mixed with breadcrumbs and a little seasoning. Place pheasants in large pot-roast container, pour over ½ pint of the marinade, herbs and all. Add to the pot the mushrooms, celery, onions and a little seasoning.

Cook slowly in a medium oven until it smells so delicious that it must be done. I usually lower the heat right down at this stage and really let the dish cook on to increase the flavour. At this point you can serve the dish as it is, for some of the bread will have leaked out of the birds' stuffing during the cooking process and will have added its own thickening agent to the stock. But if you prefer a clear sauce, remove the birds from the pot and strain the sauce into a new saucepan. Reduce the stock by one third by rapid boiling without a lid. Pour the gravy sauce back over the cooked birds and garnish with a few whole raspberries and serve.

Yes, the raspberries do disintegrate and fall out of the birds during the cooking process, but while they have been cooking they have added their own special flavour to the juices of the meat; besides they don't all fall out, there are usually enough left in the pheasant to serve up as an attractive stuffing.

Raspberry Ice-cream with Raspberry Wine

A punnet of fresh or frozen raspberries (raspberries freeze very well)
½ pint fresh Jersey cream, whipped
4 tablespoons sugar syrup (this can be made in bulk and kept for ice-cream making. Simply boil equal amounts of sugar and water together without stirring until the liquid becomes thick enough to drip off a spoon. Cool and store in airtight jar. It will keep for months if stored at an even temperature.)
¼ pint raspberry wine
1 fresh orange

Place raspberries and wine into the liquidizer and mix for a few moments until the raspberries have all broken up. Mix the raspberries into the cream and squeeze in the juice from the orange. Add sugar syrup and taste. You are aiming for a mixture which is slightly sweeter than you would wish it to be, for when frozen the mix will tend to taste slightly sharper than it is. As the sweetness and the thickness of your sugar syrup may vary from batch to batch, don't be ashamed of tasting and adjusting the flavours at this point. It might, for instance, need a little more orange juice to make it sharper, or even a little more wine.

If you are lucky enough to have an ice-cream maker, simply pour the mixture in and leave until set. If, however, you only have a deep freeze, pour the mixture into a shallow tray and freeze until almost firm, then take it out and whisk it up and return to the freezer. You can repeat this process twice more if you wish, but once is normally enough. Serve when frozen with sweet biscuits and a raspberry garnish.

Note that most fresh fruits make good ice-creams and sorbets. This recipe works equally well with strawberries, blackcurrants, mulberries and other soft fruits. Simply choose a wine that complements the fruit, and taste as you mix.

REDCURRANT

Redcurrant Wine

4 lb redcurrants
4 lb sugar
1 gallon water
½ oz yeast

There's no need to strip every stalk off your fruit. Place the currants in your wine-making bucket and pour over the gallon of boiling water. Cover with a cloth and leave for 4 or 5 days, stirring daily and once or twice crush the fruit with a potato masher. Now strain and tip the liquor back into your wine-making bucket, add the sugar and stir well, sprinkle on the yeast and cover again, keeping the wine in a warmish place. Leave for a week, strain off, pour into your demijohn, fix the airlock, and proceed as on page 4.

Wild Duckling Breasts Cooked in Redcurrant Wine

1 duck breast for each person
½ pint redcurrant wine
8 oz fresh or frozen redcurrants (redcurrants freeze well so
    don't be worried about using frozen fruit for this dish)
8 oz mushrooms, chopped fine
4 large tomatoes, skinned and chopped fine
Large handful parsley, chopped fine
3 sticks celery, chopped fine
3 sprigs thyme and 3 marjoram, chopped fine
3 cloves of garlic, crushed or chopped fine
2 tablespoons tomato paste
Few drops soy sauce
Flour to dust duck breasts before frying and to thicken sauce
2 tablespoons sunflower oil to fry breasts
Freshly ground black peppercorns and salt to season

Heat the oil in a shallow frying pan and fry duck breasts which have been dusted with seasoned flour. Carefully turn the breasts and fry until they are golden brown but not cooked through. Remove duck breasts from the pan and place in a casserole dish on top of half the redcurrants. Lower the heat of the remaining oil and juices and add the tomatoes, mushrooms, garlic, parsley, thyme, marjoram and celery and cook very gently until soft but not brown.

Stir in the tomato paste, then add a small quantity of flour to this mix (about 1 tablespoon should be enough). Stir in, and gradually add the wine, stirring throughout. If the mix is still thick when all the wine has been added, put in a drop more until you have a reasonably thin sauce. Add soy sauce. Season and spoon this mixture over the duck breasts. Place remaining redcurrants on top and cook in a medium-to-low oven for at least an hour. Check for seasoning and serve.

You can add a few small onions to this dish if you wish. I made it without them the first time and was so satisfied with the finished flavour I have never bothered to add them.

RHUBARB

Rhubarb Wine

Don't use very young rhubarb for this wine, and don't leave it till the stalks are hard and tough – late May or early June should be about the right time. An old lady once told me, 'Don't make yer rhubarb wine till the leaves be as big as an elephant's ear.' You will need

> *4 lb rhubarb*
> *3 lb 8 oz sugar*
> *1 gallon water*
> *½ oz yeast*
> *A piece of root ginger as big as a walnut*

Wipe the rhubarb with a cloth and cut it into small pieces – don't peel it. Pour over a gallon of boiling water, add the ginger, cover and leave for 4 days, stirring each day. Strain, add the sugar, stir until dissolved, then sprinkle on the yeast, cover and leave for a further 2 days. Then strain off into your demijohn and proceed as on page 4. This is a semi-sweet wine, lovely served with ice on hot summer evenings. Drinkable after 6 months – watch out, though, it's supposed to be an aphrodisiac.

Orange Slices Spiced with Rhubarb Wine

4 firm oranges, peeled with all pith removed and sliced thin,
*   cutting through segments to produce perfect even circles of*
*   fruit*
½ pint rhubarb wine
6 cloves
2 sticks cinnamon
6 allspice
1 oz fresh ginger, chopped fine

Place cloves, cinnamon, allspice and fresh ginger into small muslin bag for easy removal later. Pour the wine into a medium-sized frying pan with lid and carefully lay orange slices in the wine. Place the muslin bag of spices into the wine so that they are well covered and simmer with lid on for 10 minutes on a very low heat, just enough to release the aromatic spice flavours but not enough to spoil the shape of the orange slices.

Turn off the heat and allow the ingredients to stand for at least 2 hours. Remove the spice bag and place the orange slices into an attractive dish and serve when chilled right through. A garnish of thinly sliced orange peel boiled for a moment or two in a drop of wine will enhance this dish. It is also very nice garnished with thin cracked toffee on top.

ROSEHIP

Rosehip Wine

September and October are the best months to make this wine. I use the hips of the wild dog-rose, but I suppose rosehips from the garden would do just as well. Rosehips are full of vitamin C and make a delicious deep rosé-wine.

> *3 lb rosehips (gathered after the first frost of autumn)*
> *1 orange*
> *3 lb sugar*
> *1 gallon water*
> *½ oz yeast*

Wipe the fruit over by rolling them in a dry tea-towel. Chop them roughly in half, put into your wine-making bucket and add the sugar. Pour boiling water over them. Cover and leave for a couple of days, stirring twice daily and crushing them against the side of the bucket with a wooden spoon, or a potato masher. Now add the juice from the orange and sprinkle on the yeast. Cover and leave in a warm room for a further week. Strain, pour the liquid into the demijohn, and proceed as on page 4. Use 2 oz of dried figs, first soaked in water to plim them up, and added at the beginning of the recipe, to give a little more 'body' to the wine. The wine is drinkable within 3 months.

Chicken Breasts Stuffed with Rosehips and Rosehip Wine

4 chicken breasts, boned and skinned
1 cup rosehip wine
4 oz dried apricots, chopped fine
4 oz hazelnuts, chopped fine (almost to a powder)
Small amount parsley and fresh thyme, chopped fine
8 oz rosehips cut open, with pips removed (yes, this is a
  laborious task, but it's worth it)
1 cup chicken stock (if you use a stock cube, remember to
  reduce seasoning)
Sunflower oil to fry chicken breasts
Flour to dust chicken breasts
Freshly ground black peppercorns and salt to season

Cut into each chicken breast, but do not cut in half and press out so that the chicken flesh can be stuffed and rolled later. Prepare stuffing by poaching half of the rosehips in the wine until soft; strain and retain the wine. When cool enough, chop poached rosehips fine. Add half the chopped apricots, and all the hazelnuts, parsley and thyme. Mix these ingredients with a little of the reserved wine used for poaching the rosehips until a workable stuffing consistency is achieved. Season according to your taste.

Place a tablespoon of stuffing onto each chicken breast, roll and secure with string, tied in a way which will allow it to be easily removed later. Flour the chicken bundles and season well. Fry gently in hot oil until golden brown on all sides, then place in casserole dish. Add a little flour to the oil and juices remaining in the frying pan to form a roux, then stir in the chicken stock and wine in equal amounts. Add the remaining rosehips and apricots to the sauce, allow to bubble for a moment then pour over the chicken breasts.

Cook in a moderate oven for at least an hour. Adjust seasoning and serve with jacket potatoes and a nice autumn cabbage.

ROSE PETAL

Two Rose Petal Wines

(1)

This can be made all through the summer. There is no need to pick the roses when they are at their best – wait until they are just about to fall, so you are only saving them from the compost heap.

This is a most delightful and delicate wine, unlike any other; it will bring a breath of summer to a wintertime meal. Red rose petals are the best, and the more heavily scented they are the better, but a mixture of red, pink and yellow petals will make a nicely coloured wine.

> *2 quarts rose petals*
> *3 lb sugar*
> *1 lemon*
> *1 orange*
> *1 gallon water*
> *½ oz yeast*
> *A handful of raisins*

Place the rose petals in your wine-making vessel and pour over the boiling water. Stir well and leave for 2 days, covered. Strain and add the chopped raisins, the juice of the lemon and orange, and the sugar, and stir well. Sprinkle on the yeast, cover and leave for 2 days. Then strain again, pour into your demijohn, and proceed as on page 4.

The wine will be drinkable within 6 months, but even better by the time the roses bloom the following year. Lovely served at a summer luncheon party.

(2)

2 quarts rose petals (the stronger scented and brighter
* coloured the better)*
2 lb 8 oz sugar
1 lemon
1 gallon water
½ oz yeast

Bring the water to the boil, add the sugar, rose petals and juice of
the lemon, and stir well. When it has cooled, add the yeast. Leave
to ferment for a week, stirring daily and keeping closely covered.
Then strain into a demijohn and proceed as on page 4.

Both rose petal wines have a delicate bouquet, are slightly
scented, and are pale pinky amber in colour.

Fresh Trout with Rose Petal Wine

4 fresh trout
½ pint rose petal wine
Enough fresh rose petals to stuff the fish and garnish (these
  can be taken from the rose bush at the point just before
  they fall naturally, so you are only depriving your
  garden of blooms that the wind will claim during that
  day)
Handful fresh tarragon, chopped fine
Handful fresh chervil, chopped fine
Handful fresh parsley, chopped fine
Freshly ground black peppercorns and salt to season

Wash and prepare the trout and place each one on a square of tinfoil large enough to fold into a package while cooking. Reserve sufficient rose petals for garnish and mix the rest with the tarragon, chervil and parsley, toss lightly together and season well. Stuff the rose petals and herbs into each fish. Bring the sides of the tinfoil up so that you can add wine to each fish without it pouring all over the kitchen. Place on a tray with sides sufficient to hold any wine which may escape. Pour wine onto each fish package and fold carefully to make a sealed parcel, after seasoning.

Cook gently for about 20 minutes in a moderate oven or until the flesh feels soft but does not disintegrate when touched. Unpack the fish carefully and serve after spooning a little of the sauce onto each fish. This dish is superb served hot, but can also be served cold, with a salad mixed with a dressing made from the sauce and a little sunflower oil mixed together and seasoned, and garnished with rose petals.

Although highly perfumed, rose petal wine usually has a very dry finish, making it an ideal wine to use for any fish cookery.

RUNNER BEAN

Runner Bean Wine

You can make this wine from July until September.

> 4 lb runner beans
> 2 lemons
> 4 oz raisins
> 3 lb sugar
> 1 gallon water
> 2 tablespoons strong tea leaves
> $\frac{1}{2}$ oz yeast

Cut the beans in half and place in a saucepan. Add the lemon rinds and water, bring to the boil and simmer for 15 minutes. Strain and pour the liquid over the sugar, the juice of the lemons, the roughly chopped raisins and the tea leaves. Leave to cool, and then sprinkle on the yeast. Cover well and leave for 3 days. Strain again, tip into demijohn and proceed as on page 4.

This wine is drinkable after 4 months.

OLD WIVES' TALE: if your wine will not clear add a tablespoon of whipped white of an egg to it.

Bean Cassoulet with Runner Bean Wine

1 lb 8 oz runner beans (if you only have stringy ones don't bother to make up this dish, for you are looking for beans freshly picked and so tender that they almost melt in the pot)

½ pint runner bean wine

1 lb fresh tomatoes, skinned and chopped very fine

4 oz flageolet beans, soaked overnight in runner bean wine

4 oz chick peas, soaked overnight in runner bean wine

4 oz adzuki beans, soaked overnight in runner bean wine

1 bunch spring onions, chopped fine

4 oz mushrooms, chopped so fine that they almost vanish

8 rashers of streaky bacon with rind removed, chopped roughly

1 bunch parsley, chopped fine

2 sprigs summer savory if available, chopped fine

1 bay leaf

2 cloves garlic, chopped fine

1 cup vegetable stock (if you use a cube remember to adjust seasoning, otherwise the dish often tastes too salty)

3 dessertspoons walnut oil (if you haven't any, don't worry, sunflower oil will do. It's just that walnut oil has a very distinctive taste which goes well with this dish)

Freshly ground black peppercorns and salt to season

Drain off the wine from the beans and retain the liquid. Heat the walnut oil in a large frying pan for which you have a lid, and add the beans, the bacon bits and the garlic, and season. Gently fry ingredients together but do not brown. To this mix add the chopped mushrooms, parsley, summer savory, bay leaf, and tomatoes and cook for a little longer. Add vegetable stock and the wine that you used to soak the beans and stir well; adjust seasoning.

Allow this mix to gently simmer away with lid on for at least an hour or until the beans have cooked. In a separate pan of salted water, cook the runner beans which you have sliced in the normal way. When the runner beans are cooked, and only moments before serving, strain them well and stir them into the main mix.

You are aiming to preserve their distinct summer flavour while offering the taste-buds a complete contrast through the rest of the ingredients. Serve as a light supper dish with rice, or chunks of crusty bread, or as a side dish of vegetables to a very simple main dish.

SAGE

Sage Wine

One of the most valuable wines for those suffering from anaemia, and a delicious wine into the bargain.

> 1 lb sage leaves
> 1 lb raisins
> 3 lb demerara sugar
> 1 gallon water
> ½ oz yeast

Remove any stalks from the sage and put it into your wine-making bucket. Add the chopped raisins and the sugar. Cover with the gallon of water, which has been boiled and cooled. Stir until the sugar has dissolved and then add the yeast. Cover and leave for 4 days, stirring twice a day. Then strain, pour into the demijohn, and continue as on page 4.

A glass of this wine will aid the digestion, and help to clear the blood. (A bread-and-butter sandwich filled with sage will greatly help a person suffering from flatulence.) Drinkable after 6 months.

Vegetarian Pasties Flavoured with the Merest Touch of Sage Wine

The ingredients for this dish can vary according to the vegetables you have on hand. However, if you cook this dish during the summer the following items should be available to you.

1 tablespoon sunflower oil
8 medium new potatoes, diced quite small
1 medium onion, diced small
4 medium-sized new carrots, diced small
8 pods broad beans, shelled
8 pods peas, shelled
An assortment of fresh herbs including parsley, thyme, marjoram, chervil, summer savory and just a little lovage, all chopped fine
Mint to flavour new potatoes
Small amount sugar or honey to sweeten carrots
A very small drop sage wine to flavour pasties
Enough shortcrust pastry to make four large pasties (I find that 4 oz flour and 2 oz margarine are usually sufficient for this number, but much depends on how thick you like your pastry)
Sesame seeds to decorate finished pasties
Egg beaten well to wash over pastry before cooking
Freshly ground black peppercorns and salt to season

In a small saucepan cook up the potatoes and mint in freshly salted water, and in another cook the carrots adding a little honey or sugar to sweeten them. (Providing the broad beans and peas are young enough and tender, they should not require extra cooking.) Strain off carrots and potatoes when cooked. Pour a tablespoon of sunflower oil into the frying pan to which you add potatoes and carrots, and all the remaining vegetables. Season and cook for just a few moments over a moderate heat to allow the peas and broad beans to be exposed to heat and to cook slightly. Add herbs to the dish and a *very* small amount of sage wine – a few drops too many and you will drown the delicate flavours of the summer veget-ables.

Set the mixture to one side to cool slightly while you prepare the shortcrust pastry in the normal way. When the dough has been made, roll out the pastry and cut 4 rounds using a saucer as a guide. Brush egg wash around the top outer rim of each round to permit a good seal when the rims are squeezed together. Fill each round with the vegetable mix, seal and decorate with egg wash and sesame seeds. Bake in a moderate oven until golden brown and serve hot with crisp green vegetables and new potatoes.

Pork Chops with Sage Wine Sauce

4 pork chops
4 sprigs fresh sage, chopped coarsely
2 dessertspoons sage wine
½ pint rich brown stock
2 medium onions cut very fine
4 oz mushrooms, chopped very fine
4 sprigs parsley, chopped fine
3 tablespoons sunflower oil to fry
Flour to dust chops
Freshly ground black peppercorns and salt to season

Trim the chops by cutting away any surplus fat, and dust with seasoned flour. Heat the oil in a frying pan large enough to take all four chops at once. Fry the chops until golden brown and cooked right through. Remove chops from the frying pan and keep warm.

To the remaining oil and juices add the mushrooms and onions and cook through until golden brown, adding the chopped parsley at the end. Raise the heat a little and add the brown stock and bring to the boil and keep bubbling for a few moments while it reduces by at least a third. Pour in the wine and continue to cook at a moderate heat for a few more moments.

Check flavour and seasoning – you should have a subtle sage-flavoured mix that is just slightly sweet but not overpoweringly so. Toss in the chopped sage leaves, stir them in, pour sauce over the cooked chops and serve.

SLOE

Sloe Wine

This wine is best made in October when there has been a frost or two – the sloes show up on the bushes because by then most of the leaves have fallen off.

The recipe was given to me many years ago by an elderly lady who lived in the village. Her cottage was so small that she had to keep her wine on the stairs, and they were those twisty stairs at that. On every step there were bottles of wine. 'We 'as to be a bit careful when we goes to bed,' she told me, 'specially when we've been drinking some o' my ten-year-old.'

> 3 lb sloes
> 1 gallon boiling water
> 4 lb sugar (if you want it dry, add less)
> $\frac{1}{2}$ oz yeast
> 2 wineglasses of brandy

Pick off any stalks and wipe the sloes in a clean tea-towel. Place them in your wine-making vessel and pour the boiling water over them. Cover and leave for 5 days, stirring daily, lightly crushing the sloes against the side of the container with a wooden spoon. Then strain, add the sugar and stir. Add the yeast, cover again and leave for a week. Tip all into your demijohn and continue as on page 4. When bottling off, divide 2 wineglasses of brandy between the bottles.

Try and leave it for a year, if you can. This makes a strong, full-bodied wine, rich and red, lovely served with pheasant or good English beef.

Sloe Pancakes

Pancakes
4 oz plain flour
1 egg
½ pint milk

Sauce
Rind of 1 lemon
1 orange, halved and ready to squeeze
1 tablespoon caster sugar
2 oz butter
½ pint sloe wine
Dash sloe gin

Filling
8 oz sloes
A little caster sugar perhaps to sweeten (a matter of taste)

Make pancakes in advance (the day before if you wish), by placing flour into a bowl and beating in first the egg and then the milk by degrees, whisking at each stage to remove lumps. Let this mixture stand for at least 2 hours. Whisk again and establish you have a smooth batter. Cook pancakes in the traditional way, using very little oil and a very hot pan. They can be placed one on top of each other and saved – you should get at last 2 for each person from this mix. Remove the pips from the sloes, a task which takes time and is best done either in a relaxed manner in front of the fire listening to some good music, or by removing pips after the sloes are cooked.

Poach sloes in a little of their own wine until tender. Strain off when cooked and retain the juices. Set sloes to one side. Complete the dish only when you are ready to serve it, for it is best fresh even if it means leaving your guests to chat among themselves while you vanish into the kitchen. Using a large shallow pan, heat the butter but do not allow it to brown – add sugar and stir. When the sugar and butter begin to caramelize add a touch of sloe gin – with *great* care for it may ignite and produce a flambé effect which is an ideal flavour enhancer but not too good if you have a low ceiling. Immediately squeeze the juice from the orange into this mix and add lemon rind; stir well. Add a generous slurp of wine and allow to simmer; add the rest of the wine and reduce the liquid by at least a third.

Place the first pancake into this liquid, filling the centre with a spoonful of sloes and if needed a touch of sugar. Fold the pancake in half and then in half again and move to one side of the pan. The liquid should still be bubbling but not furiously. Repeat the process with the next pancake and then next. Don't panic when the pan begins to fill, it's possible to get 8 pancakes in one by one and actually fold them too – just take it easy and you will manage to do it.

When all the pancakes are folded and soaking up the liquid, serve in the pan at the table. (Only dish them up in the kitchen if you really must, for the effect of a panful of hot juicy pancakes is superb and well worth showing to your guests.)

STRAWBERRY

Strawberry Wine

Make this whenever strawberries are available.

If you are like me and pick more than you really need at those 'pick-your-own' farms, it's a good idea to use the very best fruit for jam-making or eating and the rest to make delicious wine.

> 4 lb strawberries
> 1 gallon water
> 3 lb sugar
> Juice of 2 lemons
> $\frac{1}{2}$ oz yeast
> A wineglass of whisky

Place the fruit in the wine-making vessel and mash against the side with a wooden spoon. Then pour over the cold water and leave covered for 2 days. Strain and add the lemon juice and the sugar. Stir well before adding the yeast. Cover and leave for 4 days before straining off into your demijohn. Proceed as on page 4. When you bottle this wine off, a wineglass of whisky divided between the bottles will help to produce a super wine.

The wine should be ready to drink in 6 months.

Strawberry Trifle Made with Fresh Strawberries and Strawberry Wine

2 punnets fresh strawberries (more if you want to make a really special dish)

1 pint custard made to your favourite recipe

4 trifle sponges

3 teaspoons strawberry jam

¼–½ pint strawberry wine (quantity will depend on how sloppy you want the finished dish to be)

1 teaspoon arrowroot

½ pint fresh Jersey cream

Place the trifle sponges in the bottom of an attractive glass dish and break up slightly. Spoon in the jam and mix into the sponges. Add half the strawberries, and mix with the sponges, placing as many as possible round the side of the dish so that they can be seen through the glass. Pour on as much strawberry wine as you think the sponges will take. Pour on a pint of custard and leave to cool while you whip the cream. Add the whipped cream to the dish, layering it on top of the cool custard. Pile the rest of the strawberries on top of the cream in an attractive way.

Bring 4 dessertspoons of wine to the boil and add the arrowroot which has been thinned with a little wine, stir well and remove from the heat when the mix has thickened. When the sauce is cool simply pour it over the strawberries on top of trifle so that it runs where it wants to. This adds not only a superb gloss to the finished dish, but looks very attractive if it is allowed to run into the cream. If it goes over the sides of the glass dish, don't worry, you can either leave it like that or wipe the dish clean.

As fresh strawberries are available at a price during December I make this trifle every Christmas. It has become a firm favourite with the family who love the idea of enjoying a taste of the summer during the festive season.

TEA

Two Tea Wines

(1)

4 tablespoons dry tea leaves
Juice and rind of 1 lemon
2 lb 8 oz sugar
1 gallon water
½ oz yeast

Some of the scented Indian and China teas make lovely, clear, dry wines. Pour the boiling water over the tea and sugar, stir well, and leave until cool. Add the juice and rind of a lemon and the yeast, cover and leave for 2 days, strain and pour into the demijohn. Fit an airlock, and proceed as on page 4.

Because this wine does not have the bouquet of other wines, it is a good one for blending with, say, a very dry wine, but don't do this until you are ready to drink it – which should be 6 months after you have made it.

(2)

1 gallon tea (any type will do)
1 lb raisins
4 lb sugar
Juice of 4 lemons
Juice of 2 grapefruit
1 oz yeast

Save any left-over tea from the teapot until you have collected a gallon. Strain off any leaves. Add the sugar and the lemon and grapefruit juice to the liquid. Stir well till all the sugar has dissolved. Chop up the raisins and add them also, along with the yeast. Cover and leave in the warm for 5 days. Strain off, pour into the demijohn, and proceed as on page 4. Drinkable after 6 months.

Crispy Roast Duck with Honey and Tea Wine

The first tea wine recipe is best for this dish.

1 fresh duck
2 dessertspoons of runny honey
2 dessertspoons of soy sauce
2 dessertspoons tea wine, or any light wine which has acquired a sherry-like flavour
1 large onion, peeled but not chopped
Freshly ground black peppercorns and salt to season

Wash duck and place on a rack fitted over a large roasting tray. Shake honey, soy sauce and wine together to form a good mix. Brush duck all over with mix, inside and out, and place onion inside for extra flavour (this will be removed before serving). Keep back unused honey mix for further bastings. Gently cook duck in moderate heat, basting with the honey mix at 15-minute intervals. The duck will turn golden brown quite quickly as honey is exposed to heat, so check the flesh as well as the duck's colour before declaring it done. It should take about 1½ hours, depending on size.

Remove the duck from the tray and keep warm while you take the fat off the juices in the bottom of the pan. I find that this is best done with a soup spoon, or any large spoon with a reasonably flat surface. When all the fat has been removed, place the remaining juices over a moderate heat and allow them to reduce in volume a little. Adjust seasoning – you are aiming for a savoury sauce that has within it just a hint of sweetness. The sauce can be thickened with arrowroot if you wish, though I prefer serving it over the carved meat just as it is.

Serve with new potatoes and a simple green vegetable for the best balance of flavours.

155

Prunes in Tea Wine

1 lb prunes, the type that require soaking overnight
½ pint tea wine
Sugar optional, depending on your taste

Simply soak the prunes in the tea wine overnight in a cool place.
Next day, place the whole mix into a saucepan and gently poach
the prunes until soft and cooked. (Add sugar to this if you feel it
needs some – it really is a matter of taste.) Serve hot or cold with
cream or yoghurt.

WALLFLOWER

Wallflower and Grapefruit Wine

4 quarts wallflower heads
2 grapefruit
1 gallon boiling water
½ oz yeast

Measure the flowerheads in a quart jug, press the flowers down well, tip them into your wine-making bucket along with the sliced grapefruit. Cover and leave for a week. Strain, tip the juice back in the bucket and add the sugar, stirring well. When cool add the yeast, cover well and leave for about a week before straining off and tipping into your demijohn. Fix the airlock and proceed as on page 4.

This is a brand new recipe – the colour is a lovely golden but I have yet to taste it.

WALNUT

Walnut Leaf Wine

You can make this wine in early spring, when the leaves are young and green, or in late July when they are beginning to turn yellow.

> *1 gallon walnut leaves (loosely packed in a measuring jug)*
> *3 lb sugar*
> *Juice of 2 lemons*
> *8 oz honey*
> *1 gallon water*
> *$\frac{1}{2}$ oz yeast*

Bring the water to the boil and dissolve the sugar and honey in it. When this clears, pour it boiling over the leaves. Infuse overnight. The next day, strain and add the lemon juice, and yeast. Cover and leave for 2 or 3 days. Strain, tip into your demijohn and continue as on page 4.

This will make a delicate light wine with a subtle flavour; it should be drinkable in 3 months.

Avocado Chicken with Walnut Leaf Wine Cream Sauce

4 chicken breasts
¼ pint walnut leaf wine
2 oz unsalted butter
¼ pint single cream
2 tablespoons flour
1 oz paprika
½ pint milk
2 large ripe avocados
Freshly ground black peppercorns and salt to season

Melt the butter in a large frying pan and add the chicken portions, which have been dusted with a little seasoned flour, and cook on both sides until golden brown. Add the wine and bring to the boil then reduce the heat and allow to simmer for at least 30 minutes. Remove the chicken joints from the pan and keep in a warm place while you prepare the sauce. Allow the liquid left in the pan to cool, then mix in the flour and paprika.

Gradually add the milk, stirring all the time to achieve a smooth sauce. Add the cream when the sauce has taken all the milk and adjust seasoning. Peel the avocados and slice like orange segments – don't cut them too thin or they may break up as you heat them through. Place the avocado into the sauce and allow to bubble for a moment or two. Either add the chicken portions to the pan or pour the sauce over each portion.

Watercress makes an ideal garnish for this dish and watercress and orange salad goes well as an accompaniment.

WHEAT AND RAISIN

Wheat and Raisin Wine

You can make this wine any time after the grain harvest is in. I often wait until January or February to make mine.

> *1 lb wheat (cadged from a farmer)*
> *1 lb chopped raisins*
> *1 lb chopped and peeled old potatoes*
> *4 lb sugar*
> *1 gallon water*
> *1 oz yeast*

Put the wheat, chopped raisins, potatoes and sugar into your wine-making bucket and cover with a gallon of *boiled* cold water. Sprinkle on the yeast, cover with a cloth and leave for 2 weeks. Stir gently once a day with a wooden spoon. Strain, pour into the demijohn, and proceed as on page 4.

This makes a wonderful wine which tastes and looks almost like whisky, and can be drunk after 6 months.

> *Let us have wine and women, mirth and laughter,*
> *Sermons and soda-water the day after*
>
> LORD BYRON (1788–1824)

Chocolate Cheesecake with Wheat and Raisin Wine

8 oz digestive biscuits, crumbled fine
6 oz unsalted butter
3 tablespoons golden syrup
1 lb cream cheese, beaten until smooth
3 eggs, separated
2 oz plain chocolate (much depends upon the flavour of the
  chocolate so buy a good kind)
3 drops vanilla essence
8 oz caster sugar
2 teaspoons wheat and raisin wine
2 tablespoons powdered gelatine
½ pint rich Jersey cream, whipped until it holds its shape
Pinch salt to bring out flavour

Melt 4 oz of butter and 2 tablespoons of the golden syrup together in a saucepan and heat gently until the butter has melted and they have mixed together well. Stir into this mix the crushed biscuits and stir until the butter and syrup have been absorbed. Press this mix into a greased tin, which will allow easy removal later, and cool. Place the rest of the butter and syrup and the chocolate into a bowl which is large enough to fit over a saucepan of boiling water securely. Allow the chocolate to melt, add vanilla essence and stir until you have a fine glossy mixture. Beat the egg yolks into the cream cheese in another bowl, adding sugar and wine to achieve a smooth mix.

Soften the gelatine in about 4 tablespoons of cold water by sprinkling it over the water until it has begun to dissolve. Bring this gelatine mix to a warm temperature in the same way you softened the chocolate over hot water, stirring until all the gelatine has dissolved. This takes time, but it's worth the effort. Whisk the egg whites until they are stiff. Now you mix the whole lot together – the cooled gelatine to the cream cheese mix, then the cream, and finally the egg whites.

Pour the mix onto the biscuit crust, then quickly decorate the top with the melted chocolate mix. This can be done by spooning it on in lines, or pouring it on gently from a cream jug. Either way, you are aiming to cover the top in an attractive but casual manner so that it looks as good as it tastes.

Chill the cheesecake until set and cut only when completely cool and firm.

Cool Drinks
for
Warm Nights
and
Hot Days

Many of these drinks can be made using your home-made wines so they are quite cheap to produce.

Apple Dash

1 bottle home-made apple wine (see page 13)
1 lb sliced peaches (tinned peaches will do)
2 small glasses of brandy
1 bottle fizzy lemonade
Sugar
Ice

Put the sliced peaches in a bowl and cover with the apple wine and brandy. Leave for 2 hours. Just before serving add sugar to taste, then the lemonade and ice.

Apple Drink

5 or 6 big cooking apples
1 lemon
2 large cups of water
8 oz sugar

Slice the cooking apples thinly – don't peel them or remove the cores. Put the sliced apples in a saucepan, together with the rind and juice of the lemon and the cups of water. Cook until soft and then add the sugar. Leave to get cold, then strain. A refreshing drink, and very good for sufferers from constipation. Dilute if necessary.

Cherry Cheer

1 bottle sweet red home-made wine (sloe or blackcurrant,
  see pages 148, 34)
1 bottle parsley brandy wine (see page 112)
4 tablespoons cherry brandy
1 lb stoned cherries
Sugar to taste
Ginger ale
Ice

Pour all the liquids over the cherries. Add sugar to taste. Chill for
an hour in the fridge and serve with ice and ginger ale.

Cucumber Cobbler

1 medium-size cucumber
4 tablespoons caster sugar
1 lemon
3 tablespoons brandy
½ pint white wine (elderflower is nice, see page 68)
1 bottle red wine (blackberry would do, see page 30)
Soda water
Ice

Thinly slice the cucumber and place in a bowl along with the juice
of the lemon and the peel (very thin). Cover with the sugar and
mash all together with a wooden spoon. Add the brandy and the
red and white wines. Cover bowl with a tea-towel, and put it in
the fridge for an hour. Before serving add the ice and soda water.
Remove the lemon peel at the last moment.

Dandelion Summer Drink

3 quarts dandelion petals
2 lb sugar
1 gallon water
2 lemons

Put the dandelion petals, lemon rinds and water into a large saucepan. Simmer together for 30 minutes, topping up with water to make up for any boiling away. Strain and add the sugar and lemon juice and stir well. Bottle off. This will not keep for very long, but it is best kept in the fridge once you have started on a bottle. Lovely served with ice cubes on a very hot day.

Elderberry Water

A delightful and refreshing drink for children. You require

1 lb ripe elderberries
Sugar to taste (about 8 oz)
Juice of a lemon
Boiling water

Strip the stalks from the elderberries. Put the elderberries ina quart jug, and add the sugar and the juice of the lemon. Top up with boiling water. Stir and leave to get cold. Strain through muslin and squeeze out all the liquid. This will keep for 5 or 6 days, quite well.

Elderflower Champagne

3 heads of elderflowers (no green)
1 lb 8 oz caster sugar
2 tablespoons white wine vinegar
1 lemon
1 gallon water

Put the blossoms into a bowl or bucket. Sprinkle over the lemon juice and the grated rind, along with the sugar and wine vinegar. Add a gallon of cold water. Cover and leave for 24 hours. Strain into bottles and leave for 2 weeks before drinking, when it should be clear and sparkling. This is a delightful refreshing summer drink but will only keep for a matter of a few weeks – through the hot summer weather. Store the bottles on their side in a cool place.

Elderflower Champagne Cordial

25 elderflower heads (no green)
4 oranges
3 lb sugar
4 pints water
1 lemon
2 oz tartaric acid

Boil the water and leave until cool. Then pour this over the elderflowers, the sugar, the tartaric acid and the finely sliced oranges and lemon. Leave for 48 hours, then strain and bottle off. Use diluted. A delightful summer drink.

Harvesters' Drink

1 lemon
1 grapefruit
1 orange
1 gallon water
4 oz fine oatmeal

Grate the rinds from the fruit and then put them into a saucepean.
Add the juice from the fruit, along with the oatmeal and sugar and
2 pints of water. Bring to the boil and simmer for 10 minutes,
stirring. Take off the heat and add the rest of the water. Stir well,
strain when cold. A refreshing harvest-time drink.

Midsummer Magic

If you are having guests for luncheon or dinner, this drink will
definitely add 'magic' to the conversation.

1 bottle sweet red wine (cherry or blackberry, see pages 44,
* 30)*
1 bottle white medium-sweet wine (elderflower or dande-
* lion, see pages 68, 52)*
1 lb strawberries
1 lb raspberries
1 orange (thinly sliced)
2 sweet apples (thinly sliced)
Sugar to taste
2 tablespoons cherry brandy
Ice cubes

Put all the fruit in a large bowl and cover with all the liquids. Stir
in sugar to taste and chill. Serve with ice cubes.

Nettle Beer

This is a very wholesome drink which clears the blood and strengthens the digestion, and one that country folk relied on years before the health service. It is equally good to drink today. In spring when the green nettles are young and at their best, then's the time to make your nettle beer, and you will need

> *2 lb nettle tops (just the green tops of the nettle)*
> *2 lemons*
> *1 gallon water*
> *1 lb demerara sugar*
> *1 oz cream of tartar*
> *$\frac{1}{2}$ oz yeast*

Rinse the nettles under the tap. Put them in a saucepan with the water. Bring to the boil and simmer for 15 minutes. Then strain. Put the rind and the juice of the lemon, and the sugar and the cream of tartar, into a bowl. Stir well and add them to the liquid. Add the yeast when the liquid is cool but not cold. Cover and keep in a warm room for a couple of days. Strain into strong bottles, and don't cork too tightly; strong bottles are a 'must' – cider bottles will do – as the drink becomes gassy. Keep at least a week before drinking.

This is not a wine, so try to drink it within 3 months.

Nettle Syrup

This again is a good blood purifier, and makes a very pleasant summer drink, especially when soda water is added to it.

2 lb young nettle tops
4 pints water
Sugar (for quantity see below)

Pick the young nettle tops on a fine day, and rinse them under the tap. Put into a saucepan, along with the water. Bring to the boil and simmer for about an hour, replacing the water that has boiled away. Strain when fairly cool and add one pound of sugar to every pint of liquid. Stir well. Bottle off when cold.

Summer Special

A lunchtime treat.

1 bottle sweet red wine (blackcurrant is recommended, see
  page 34)
4 tablespoons brandy
1 lb ripe strawberries
2 bottles fizzy lemonade

Soak the strawberries in the brandy overnight, then add the wine and cool in fridge. Just before serving add the lemonade. Super!

Hot Punches
for
Cold Nights

Your guests will appreciate a drink of hot punch or mulled wine just before they go home on a cold frosty night. Here are a few ideas that are not too lethal, using your home-made wines. Serve in a strong heat-proof cup or glass.

Blackberry and Crab-apple Punch

1 pint blackberry wine (see page 30)
1 pint crab-apple wine (see page 47) or any good red wine –
  cherry, sloe or elderberry (see pages 44, 148, 58)
1 lemon (thinly sliced)
1 orange (thinly sliced)
6 cloves
1 teaspoon ground ginger
1 teaspoon mixed spice
1 teaspoon grated nutmeg
12 oz demerara sugar

Put all the ingredients into a large saucepan, and *almost* bring to the boil, stirring all the while. Strain into a punch bowl or similar container. Serve at once.

Christmas Cracker

2 pints of wine (elderberry and sloe recommended, see pages
  58, 148)
1 roasted lemon stuck with a dozen cloves
8 oz demerara sugar
1 heaped teaspoon cinnamon
2 oranges (thinly sliced)
1 extra orange

Roast the lemon stuck with cloves in a hot oven for about 30 minutes. Bring from the oven hot, and mix it with the rest of the ingredients. Put into a large saucepan and bring almost to the boil. Strain and float more slices of thinly sliced orange on the top.

Two Red Rockets

(1)

1 pint red wine (mixed fruit wine recommended, see page
 99)
1 pint white wine (elderflower or meadowsweet, see pages
 68, 95)
1 pint freshly brewed tea (any sort will do)
1 orange (thinly sliced)
1 lemon (thinly sliced)
1 large apple (thinly sliced)
12 oz demerara sugar
1 teaspoon nutmeg
1 teaspoon cinnamon
1 tin sliced peaches

Put the sugar, spices, strained tea, lemon, orange and apple into saucepan. Bring almost to the boil and simmer very gently until the sugar has dissolved. Add the wines and heat again. Strain and tip the tin of sliced peaches on top. Serve at once.

(2)

1 bottle any good home-made red wine (elderberry or
 blackberry recommended, see pages 58, 30)
1 roasted orange stuck with a dozen cloves
8 oz demerara sugar
6 tablespoons of rum

Put the orange stuck with cloves into a hot oven for about 30 minutes. Put the wine into a saucepan and bring almost to the boil. Add the rum and sugar and stir, then float the orange on the top. Serve at once.

Liqueurs

These, of course, are quite expensive, but if you have fruit in your garden and can go out and pick sloes, it is not so bad.

Blackcurrant Gin and Cherry Gin

8 oz blackcurrants
caster sugar (for quantity see below)
1 pint of gin

Remove the stalks and place the berries in a mixing bowl and crush the fruit with a large wooden spoon. Tip fruit and juice into a Kilner jar and add the gin. Screw the bottle down and leave for about 8 weeks. Then strain the liquor into a bowl and add 6 oz of sugar to each pint of juice. Cover and leave for 3 days, stirring a couple of times a day to make sure that all the sugar has dissolved. Strain and bottle the blackcurrant gin. Keep for 4 months before drinking.

Cherry gin is made by the same method as blackcurrant gin. Some people don't take the stalks off the cherries. Keep the gin-soaked cherries after straining and serve them with before-dinner drinks.

Cherry Brandy

1 lb firm ripe cherries
12 oz caster sugar
6 blanched almonds
1 pint brandy

Remove the stalks and roll the cherries in a clean tea-towel. then put alternate layers of cherries and sugar into a Kilner jar. Screw down and shake a couple of times a day for 4 days. Then add the brandy and the blanched almonds. Screw down again and leave for at least 3 months before straining, first through muslin and then through filter paper. Bottle and try to keep until Christmas. Use the brandy-soaked cherries in a trifle.

Damson Gin

1 lb damsons
1 pint gin
8 oz sugar
¼ pint sherry

Free the fruit from stalks and wipe them clean by rolling them in a tea-towel. Pierce every damson with a darning needle and drop into a large Kilner-type jar. Tip in gin, sugar and sherry over the damsons. Put the lid on and gently shake the jar once a day for a couple of weeks. Leave for a further 3 months before straining off into jars. Finally, strain through filter papers before drinking.

> *What's drinking?*
> *A mere pause from thinking*
>
> LORD BYRON (1788–1824)

Marrow Rum

1 large firm harvested marrow (don't use young green ones)
Demerara sugar
1 lb raisins
½ oz dried yeast

Cut the top off your marrow and scoop out all the seeds and soft pith. Fill the hole to the top with demerara sugar. Mix up the yeast with a tablespoon of warm water, and top the sugar up with this mixture. Put the marrow's 'lid' back on: either tie it on length-ways or stick it on with Sellotape. Stand the marrow upright in a large jug. Cover it with a cloth and keep it in a warm room. When the yeast has stopped working, strain off the liquid from the marrow and measure it. Add 1 lb of chopped raisins to each gallon of liquid. Put all into your demijohn for a week. Strain and bottle.

Orange Gin and Orange Whisky

3 oranges
2 lemons
1 pint gin
1 lb 8 oz sugar

Grate the rinds of the oranges and lemons into a bowl and then add the juice from them. Add the gin and the sugar and stir all together until the sugar has dissolved. Cover and leave for 3 weeks, stirring every day. Then strain and bottle off. The longer you can keep this the better it will be.

Orange whisky can be made in much the same way – just substitute whisky for gin.

Once you have opened a bottle of country wine, there is no need to use it all at once. Tightly corked, it will keep indefinitely, so you can take a swig when you like.

Raspberry Brandy

◇◇◇

1 lb raspberries
1 pint brandy
1 lb caster sugar
Pinch of cinnamon

Hull the fruit and put in a large jar. Pour over it the brandy and sugar and cinnamon. Cover and leave to steep in this for a month. Strain and bottle; it should be ready to drink in 6 months.

Raspberry Gin

I tried this last year for the first time, there being a glut of raspberries. Drunk at Christmas time, it made a lovely change from sloe gin or any of the more popular drinks.

2 lb raspberries
1 pint gin
1 lb sugar

Hull the fruit and put it into a stone jar together with the sugar and gin. Cover with kitchen foil. Stir for 3 or 4 days running to make sure that all the sugar has dissolved. Leave for 6 months, after which the gin will be a lovely colour and very clear. Strain off fruit (which can be used in a trifle), and bottle. Super!

Sloe Gin

1 lb sloes
6 oz caster sugar
1 pint gin

Pick all the stalks from the fruit. Prick each sloe several times with a large darning needle before dropping them into a Kilner-type jar. Add the sugar and screw the jar down. Shake the jar daily for a couple of weeks. Then add the gin and screw down again, and leave for 3 months. Strain, bottle and drink when the fancy takes you.